TELEVISION – BEHIND THE SCENES

To Sue
For Gareth

FOREWORD

It is an often held misconception that years and years of production and presentation experience in television enables a performer to embark upon a programme, and even in those final moments of countdown, suffer ne'er a trace of nerves! Let me dispel that notion immediately. The experience gained teaches one to control the inevitable tensions and fears, but they are there.

I am grateful they are too, for I'm sure that nervous tension can help give a sparkle and edge to a performance. Now the quickening pulse rate, and the resulting flow of adrenalin, is why television, for most of us who work in front and behind cameras, is an opiate.

Although most of the week on *World of Sport* may be concerned with the sheer routine of television, we couldn't exist without that weekly injection of performance. And whether that is followed by elation, because it all went well, or by disappointment, because it wasn't quite what we'd hope for – either way, the thrill of doing it is what titillates the appetite.

As I suggested, nerves are not the prerogative of a front person. The whole team share those sensations, including the director, the editor, cameramen, control room technicians and all, because they know they are going to be subjected to considerable pressure at certain times.

The occasional visitors to *World of Sport*, seeing television from behind the scenes for the first time, tell me how exciting and stimulating the atmosphere is, and how they are caught up in the tension of the live studio. We are lucky people, and Peter Jones, a colleague of mine for some time at *World of Sport*, knows this and he transmits the excitement of television, whether live or recorded, admirably in the chapters ahead. His is the widest experience, for he has probed very successfully the various areas of the medium – drama, light entertainment, sport, outside broadcast, current affairs and documentary. It would have been easy for him to surround this subject with an aura of mystery. To give the view that the business of making television is one pursued on an elevated plane. He dispels that myth from the start, and that is why, in my view, this book is long overdue!

Even after 23 years in this exciting world, I have gleaned much from its pages – about other areas of television, and particularly in the sphere of drama.

You will find the chapters on the making of that long-established serial, *Emmerdale Farm*, thoroughly absorbing, even if that is not your viewing choice! The attention to detail, the thoroughness of preparation, the rigid schedule, and the remorseless pace at which the episodes have to be written, produced and edited, imposes such disciplines on every single member of a large and caring team. It is a fascinating insight into that branch of the medium. Although it is recorded television, come recording day the atmosphere is as charged as with a live show.

Peter Jones' own great gift as a director and producer is that he can channel all the good aspects of this charge of energy into getting the maximum performance out of his crew and artistes. Although you might think from reading this book that Peter himself is on a permanent high of enthusiasm, I know so well from experience that he can also exert a very calming influence on a performer's occasionally over-stretched nerves! I have much to thank him for, and I think you will after reading this book!

Dickie Davies

INTRODUCTION

This book is an attempt to capture and convey something of the flavour of life in television. For many of us who are involved in this, the most exciting of the media, it is more than a job. Rather, it is akin to a total involvement with a capricious, demanding, but rewarding mistress. It is an involvement that can easily become an obsession.

What this book is *not* about is any attempt to explain fully, and in minute detail, the techniques by which every type of television programme is made, nor does it contain a detailed and comprehensive course on how to become a qualified video editor or make-up girl. The reasons will become obvious. So complex is the description of the work involved in the making of a fairly routine thirty-minute magazine programme, for example, that to devote the same space to every other type of TV programme (situation comedy, drama, outside broadcasts, musical spectaculars, quiz games, children's programmes and so on) would be beyond the scope of any one book of this nature.

The individual skills of cameramen, sound technicians, the special effects department, make-up, costume, editing and many other careers in television have each had whole books devoted to the complexities and techniques required to succeed in these areas. What, however, this book does try to achieve is to open the door of the world of television and thereby reveal something of the daily working life of those who have to blend their special skills with other talented people to produce an end-product which can take a multitude of forms – the television programme.

The reader will probably notice, too, that there is an indisputable bias towards the description of life in British Commercial Television rather than that in the BBC; also that certain types of programmes are given more space than others of apparently equal significance. These were deliberate and considered decisions by the author, and although I make no apology for them I feel that some explanation is deserved.

I have maintained the principle throughout that I would write only about what I *know* rather than what I *know of*. As I approach thirty years in television I am aware that I spent only two of those years at the BBC. They turned out, in many ways, to be two of the most important years of my career. Firstly, they launched me into the adventure in which I still revel. Secondly, it was during those first two years that I received the incomparable training in all aspects of television operations that only the BBC can provide, and for which I am eternally grateful. This training not only guided me through a ten-year love affair with one of the best jobs in television – camerawork – but provided me with an all-round knowledge of the work of other television professionals. You cannot be a competent cameraman unless you are aware of and sympathetic to the aims and the problems of the lighting director and the sound technician. You cannot be a good director unless you are aware of the aims and problems of *everyone* who is contributing to your programme.

The honeymoon ended, however, and I have spent the past twenty-seven years or so exclusively in ITV. It is for that reason that the book has this prejudice, for, as the opening words suggest, it is concerned with reflecting the manner of life in television on a day-to-day basis. To attempt to do this accurately the author must draw heavily on his own experience, and this I have done.

In fact, the difference between working for the BBC and working for ITV is not as marked as many people would think; there is often a greater difference between working for different ITV companies. The chapter comparing ITV's *World of Sport* and BBC's *Grandstand* (who kindly allowed me into their world as an observer) illustrates the similarities between the professional approach of those who bring these programmes to the home receiver.

Many viewers think, too, that an ITV cameraman would cross the road to avoid a BBC set designer, and that the rivalry extends to never watching the other's programmes. This is a fallacy. There might be intense competition between these two organisations at programme controller and board room level (certainly if you read the press) and there is no doubt that the 'ratings war' is here to stay, and who likes losing a war? Nevertheless, for those involved in the making of programmes there might be rivalry but little animosity. It is not at all uncommon when both BBC and ITV are covering the same event for technicians and production teams to help each other out when in difficulties, and this is a statement based on the many instances when I have benefited from and contributed to this arrangement, and know of dozens more. Quite simply, no true professional would get any satisfaction from the misfortune of another, a misfortune which might befall anyone, when all is called for is the loan of a microphone, lens, typewriter or telephone.

The structure of management and the individual responsibilities of those engaged in programme-making often differ significantly between the two organisations. The same might be said, perhaps, when comparing Woolworths and Marks and Spencers. It would be a tedious exercise in a book of this nature, however, written as it is for the average viewer, to point out continuously the different titles given by different organisations to the same job. Neither is the reader likely to be enthralled by the subtle variations in the responsibilities of individuals of different companies whose title suggests they should all be doing exactly the same job.

I hope my professional colleagues will understand, then, why I have adhered to the terminology and job-descriptions with which I am most familiar, or which I know to be in most general use. Inevitably these are associated with ITV and with the companies for whom I have worked.

In these days of non-sexual discrimination when applied to employment I have found myself on trickier ground. No longer do television companies invite applications for 'cameramen' but for 'camerapersons', and more and more women are finding careers in this formerly male-dominated world. Women are even (but whisper it) operating video tape machines in that bastion of male chauvinism. The practice has been common for many years, in fact, outside Britain, but at the time of writing it is still a little unusual. Again it would be tedious for the reader to be confronted throughout the book with phrases like 'he or she then takes his or her script to the producer who will give his or her opinion . . .' and so on *ad nauseam*. I have approached this thorny area by taking common practice as the basis for calling anyone in this book male or female.

I am not saying whether it is right or wrong that the majority of programme directors in British television are men. I neither applaud nor condemn this. *It is simply a fact of life that it is so*. It is a fact of life, too, that the vast majority of make-up artists in television are women, as are vision mixers, and production assistants. Again I express no opinion beyond reiterating that that is the way it is. Throughout the book, therefore, I have used the male or female version of any job where that job is *predominantly* carried out by one particular sex. In any case this should help the reader to understand what is going on during the description of a programme – if he knows that the director is male and the vision mixer female, then, when reading phrases such as 'he turned to her' the reader will be in no doubt as to who is turning to whom.

Some careers are shared equally by men and women. A television researcher can be from either sex, and women seem to share equal opportunities with men as producers. In those cases where there has been a choice open to me to allocate a gender to the person concerned I have tried to make the choice one way or the other in order to create a clear distinction between people engaged in the making of the programme under discussion. This is evident in the chapter on documentaries when it was fortunate, for the sake of clarity, that the researcher was a female.

Those are the only reasons for my use of male or female throughout this work. I enjoy the company of both men and women. I am neutral when it comes to sex-equality at work!

Because I have concentrated on those areas of television best known to me, it will be obvious that it is in the production of live and factual programmes that I have placed much emphasis; but there are more important reasons for this than personal choice. Television is unique compared with other forms of entertainment. It brings pictures and sound into people's homes. As we shall see later, the scope and variety of the programmes on offer is enormous and the production of these programmes makes prodigious demands on those engaged in the industry. Beyond that, though, television has another dimension which, combined with its other qualities of colour pictures and sound, leaves all its competitors in the shade. That commodity is immediacy.

Nowhere can that special ingredient be more usefully exploited to best advantage than in the area of factual programming: news, current affairs, sport and similar. And it is the making of these kinds of programmes that separates television yet further from its competitors.

Before dealing with those types of programmes, however, I wanted the reader to have a broad view of a television production. A fair proportion of the early part of this book, therefore, is devoted to the complexity of mounting a never-ending 'soap opera'. By detailing and sharing the lives of those making this type of programme it was possible to introduce a large number of television personnel encompassing a wide variety of skills and responsibilities. Even a single drama production involves contributions from almost all sections of a television company: make-up, wardrobe, and so on. An 'on-going' drama series brings further complexities, as will be evident later; but a description of such a series should enable the reader to obtain a fair grasp of the team which must be assembled to produce any major TV programme.

Only in television do we have this peculiar form of visual entertainment, the 'soap opera'; the weekly unfolding of the changing lives of a fictional group of people thrown together by circumstances, environment, way of life or type of employment. To maintain some degree of topicality these programes cannot be made too far in advance, and any outside influence which delays production can cause untold headaches for all those involved. The immediacy of television, then, exerts its influence even over the making of productions which could never be considered as factual programming.

Having looked at the drama series, it was time to move on; to move on to live and factual programmes where the immediacy of television is most apparent; to meet new people. In doing so, I am aware that I have by-passed certain other areas of television production, but this is inevitable if the reader is to be taken into fresh fields of experience.

Many viewers are now familiar with the various theatrical tricks and visual sleight-of-hand which are behind the production of films and stage plays. Indeed there have been many programmes devoted to just such revelations. The theatre has been in the business of creating make-believe for many hundreds of years, the film industry for many decades. There is little new to be unveiled as to how they achieve this.

My experience is that visitors to a television studio are invariably more intrigued and excited at being present during the transmission of a live programme than by watching the gradual assembly of a situation comedy or musical programme (apart from the opportunity to watch famous stars at close quarters). Although recorded programmes are carefully honed and polished over many months before they reach the screens in a flawless state, the same might be said of a Hollywood movie.

To understand why television is such a heady environment in which to work, to understand why it is like no other form of entertainment or media, the reader must take a deep breath and enter the adrenalin-charged world of live programmes. If this book enables anyone who reads it to experience something of the intoxication which comes from a life spent in running along that particular tight-rope then it will all have been worthwhile.

Peter Jones
1984

1 TELEVISION

Television is now so much a regular companion in most people's lives that it is inevitably taken for granted. Nothing is easier than to switch on the set, select a channel, and settle down to watch an advertised programme. And why not? That is why television was invented, to bring programmes to millions in the comfort of their own homes. Not just a random selection of programmes, of course, but a carefully prepared menu offering variety and therefore choice: programmes to entertain, inform, amuse, thrill, delight, and sometimes, perhaps, shock.

Television programmes, like everything else man-made, do not just happen; they must be made to happen. Behind the scenes, behind the screens you might say, there is a vast army of people whose lives are spent in doing just that – making programmes happen. They operate in a world which many people have glimpsed from time to time but which is largely viewed with curiosity and awe. What is it like to work in a television studio? Who is responsible for making programmes and how many people are involved? How skilled is a cameraman or make-up artist? Is the newsreader's job as easy as it looks? What is the difference between a director and a producer?

Anyone who works in television is continually bombarded with questions like these, for people *are* curious and interested. Most homes now have a television set, and an evening's viewing is a common talking point the following day. The characters in the regular 'soap operas' assume real-life qualities in the minds of millions of viewers. Yet, quite naturally, the complexities behind the making of these programmes is outside the knowledge of most people.

Let us look behind the screens, then, at the surprisingly broad variety of talents which are brought together in the making of programmes. In doing so we shall touch on many areas in television, and learn something of the specialised skills of many areas of programme-making and back-up effort. We shall look, too, at many types of programmes, although it will be impossible to include detailed descriptions of how they are made.

There is no doubt that television is a fascinating world in which to work. It is also a demanding world, hungry for inventive ideas, fresh material, new scripts. For the programmes which find their way onto television screens at home are followed by yet more programmes, day after day, year after year. Hungry and insatiable is the world of television. It is demanding in another sense, too. Whoever succeeds in television must become a skilled professional, and this expertise must be relied on, no matter how great the pressure of time or exacting the task. In addition, television often demands hard work over long hours, usually longer than the normal hours of the average shop, factory or office worker.

It is highly rewarding to the talented, the skilful and the successful; ruthless with failure, mediocrity, and those past their best. Yet for many who are part of this world it is the most thrilling and stimulating of jobs. Yes, it can be a glamorous job, too, where carpenters rub shoulders with superstars in the staff canteen and no two days are ever quite the same. For all that it is still a job.

Drive up to the crowded, giant car park of a major television company (most employees have cars for this is a well-paid industry) and it is easy to believe that this is the car park of a large industrial concern making cameras, confectionery or cars. The elegant reception area, too, with its flowers, carpets and attractive receptionists might be the entrance to a prosperous factory. Perhaps this is not surprising. Television studios are rather like large factories, producing not furniture or cornflakes but television programmes: manufacturers of make-believe.

Behind the gloss of the front office, however, the remainder of the building is designed to house the hundreds, often thousands, of busy people who contribute, in one way or another, to the whole purpose of it all – the making of television programmes. There are offices galore for directors, producers, secretaries, reporters, writers, programme planners, executives, accountants, design engineers, draughtsmen. Then there are dressing rooms for the performers, make-up rooms, the wardrobe department with its array of costumes, sewing machines and skilled dressmakers; the music section with its vast library of discs and tapes; film cutting rooms, video tape recording and editing suites, telecine machines (which transmit films), design departments where the important business of designing sets is in the hands of skilled and artistic men and women. Then there are the areas where the scenery is built, assembled, painted and stored; the Aladdin's cave of the property master, the electrical stores and workshops, the complicated electronic nerve centre; and there is much more than all that, as we shall discover.

Above all, however, there are the studios where the programmes are actually made. BBC's giant complex at the Television Centre in White City, London, has many studios of varying sizes. A small independent company like Channel TV in Jersey has just one studio; but it is adequate for their needs. Generally, however, most companies have at least two or three studios of various sizes to accommodate the different types of programmes the company makes: large studios for major plays and musical extravaganzas; smaller studios for programmes taking up

The purpose-built studios of Yorkshire Television.

less room – daily magazines, quiz shows, simple children's programmes, and such like.

Such is the demand for programmes that studios are rarely idle, particularly in major companies. As soon as one programme is transmitted or recorded the sets are removed, the 'props' placed in giant cages and wheeled away, the painting on the floor scrubbed out, and the cameras and sound equipment cleared from the centre of the floor. The studio which only an hour or so ago was filled with sets giving a realistic impression of a Victorian ballroom, the inside of the carriage of an old steam train, the servants' quarters of a stately home, and a corner of a garden in summer, now lies empty and ugly.

Empty television studios really are drab and uninspiring. The walls of bare brick are untidily covered for the most part with boxes of thick padding. These act as sound 'baffles' which deaden the sounds in the studio and reduce the echoing effect one gets in large, empty, indoor spaces. From hooks on these walls hang cables, poles and pieces of equipment. Leaning on them are ladders and odd pieces of wood and cardboard.

The floor near the base of the walls, too, is usually cluttered. Everywhere there are cables. Cables from the cameras to their connecting points on the studio walls. Cables for microphones, loudspeakers and television monitors. Cables to supply power for all sorts of uses. Then there are the cameras, maybe four or five, each mounted either on sophisticated pedestals which can be moved effortlessly and noiselessly around the studio, or on four wheeled 'cranes' which can

A fish-eye view of a complete studio set-up.

be driven around the studio by camera assistants, and which give the cameraman an exciting range of camera movement and varying heights for his shots. There are usually a couple of sound booms, too, which are three-wheeled frames on which are mounted platforms (about four feet from the ground) to support the operator. At the front of this platform a vertical pole carries a pivoted, telescopic arm. A microphone is placed at one end and the operator uses his controls to place the microphone just above the artistes as they move around the set playing their parts.

Now they stand unwanted and impotent. The whole dingy, dark and rather dirty studio seems like an ageing actress when the make-up has been taken off. From the surprisingly high ceiling the lamps which helped add such splendour to the set now hang unlit, pointing haphazardly in all directions. An empty studio is a sad sight, for these places need to be filled with sets, lights, colour, people and noise.

Within hours a transformation takes place. Where recently stood the Victorian ballroom, garden, railway carriage and servants' quarters now stands the interior of a village pub, the living room of a farmhouse and the waiting room of a veterinary surgeon. Later the same studio will be set up for a quiz game, with desks, electronic scoreboards and audience seating. No two days are alike in television, and this applies in particular to the actual studios themselves.

The broadcasting of television programmes in the United Kingdom is entrusted, of course, to two major operators, the BBC and ITV, each having two channels to carry their programmes.

The BBC was the first organisation in the world to transmit television, which it pioneered in the 1930s. Its reputation worldwide is deservedly high, and it has been responsible for training thousands of professionals who are employed in television all over the globe. The BBC carries no advertising, of course, its sole source of revenue being the annual licence fee payable by all owners of a home receiver.

Independent Television companies, the first operational in 1955, receive not a penny of this licence fee; each raises its cash by commercial means, mainly by the selling of advertising time between programmes. Fifteen companies now hold franchises under the auspices of the Independent Broadcasting Authority (the IBA) who also own the ITV transmitters for which the independent companies pay a rental. A sixteenth franchise was granted to TV-AM to provide 'breakfast television' to the network seven days a week.

Each individual company is responsible for running its own affairs, and for the provision of television programmes to its allotted area. Granada, for example, provides programmes for much of the north west of England: HTV for Wales and part of the West of England. There is an obligation on each of them to reflect local life in its programming, and to include programmes from other companies, usually done at peak viewing times in the evenings (between 6.30 and

10.30) when the whole network of fifteen companies shows the same programmes. The BBC, too, has studios throughout the main regions, and these periodically 'opt out' from the London transmission to provide programmes of local interest. These regions also contribute to national 'hook-ups', as in the early evening news magazine programme.

The cost of advertising time – the familiar commercials – varies tremendously from company to company and according to the time of day. A commercial transmitted in London at 8.30 pm during a top-rated programme costs infinitely more than a similar commercial transmitted at 3 pm to the viewers of Grampian Television. Advertisers are no fools, and they will pay big rates only if the number of prospective customers is great.

The regulations governing the screening of commercials is very strict. Cigarette advertising, for example, has been banned on ITV for some years, and there are rigid controls to ensure that commercials do not offend public taste and morals. Despite what many viewers think, there are restrictions, too, on the number and length of commercial breaks. During peak viewing time, for example, no company may screen more than seven minutes of advertisements per hour. Throughout the day the average must not be more than six minutes per hour: perhaps it just seems longer sometimes.

There are other rules also which both the BBC and ITV must abide by. Material which could be considered unsuitable for children must not be broadcast before 9 pm. There are tight restrictions on the portrayal of sex and violence, although there is a strong lobby which is not satisfied that these controls are stringent enough . . . but that would always be the case.

Political and current affairs programmes are carefully vetted to ensure that they are fair, impartial, have political balance, and respect the privacy and dignity of the individual. Around local and general elections, the time given to each of the main political parties on air is scrutinised very, very carefully to make sure that all parties have a fair and equal share of the viewers' attention.

The making of religious programmes is another area where there are tight controls which must be respected by programme-makers. In fact, all religious programmes are usually vetted and approved by a special committee before the production can be given the go-ahead. Religious and ethnic minorities are demanding and getting increased television exposure as their numbers increase. Programmes made outside the United Kingdom can occupy only a certain percentage of a TV company's schedule, and similar restrictions apply to feature films.

The impression, which many people have, that television is made by 'lefties and sweeties' just does not hold water. It is a highly professional industry employing the skills and talents of many, as we shall see. There is as much variety among the people who work in TV as there is in life itself.

2 HOW IT ALL STARTS

The main obligation of television companies is the making of television programmes, and in the case of ITV companies, also providing a regional service to the viewers in its areas. Even allowing for repeats, the amount of material consumed in the making and transmission of television programmes by one major company alone over a period of a year is prodigious. So where is the reservoir of ideas bringing fresh suggestions for programmes and novel proposals for presenting them? Who chooses between one suggestion and another? How and why do television programmes originate in the first place?

The original motivation for a programme is often quite undramatic. Within television companies the responsibility for making different kinds of programmes is broken down into a number of specialised areas, each having its own particular head of department responsible for the output of programmes in his specialised field. There is the drama department, departments specialising in sport, light entertainment, news and current affairs, children's, religious and educational programmes, documentaries, farming, science and so on.

The man at the top of the programme-making tree, the controller of programmes, is the person who ultimately decides on the overall output of his company over, say, a period of a year, and it is he who allocates to the various departments their programme-making responsibilities over the months to come. In ITV there are complicated political negotiations which have to be resolved when deciding one company's output compared with that of another, but these are, thankfully, outside the scope of this book.

More often than not, then, programmes originate when the head of documentaries, say, tells his executive producer that half-a-dozen documentaries running thirty minutes each, with a common theme of 'man against the elements', are needed for six consecutive weekly transmissions, the first to be transmitted in twelve weeks' time. There is a budget of so many thousand pounds to cover all six, so that if the making of one documentary costs more than allocated, the others must suffer financially to balance the books. Sometimes the executive producer will turn to his producers and directors and ask for suggestions, sometimes he will allocate the responsibility to one or two producers who have the 'track record' to handle this kind of assignment. In other departments, similar scenes are re-enacted.

This is when ideas are needed, and there is rarely a shortage of ideas in television both from within and outside the industry. One major ITV company receives more than two dozen scripts or synopses for plays every week, submitted by hopeful professional and amateur writers. Other departments could tell similar tales. Most of the suggestions for programmes from those outside the industry come to nothing, however. There are many reasons why. Often a suggestion for a programme is not practical in television terms: it would cost too much to make, for example, or would be too long to fit into a transmission 'slot' in a normal evening's viewing time. Many programme suggestions are simply not good enough to convert into a programme, and it is surprising how many times the same idea ends up on a producer's desk.

Suggestions for television plays are often sent to companies whose drama output per year is almost non-existent, and ideas for television spectaculars still get sent to regional companies which have neither the money, the resources, nor the time to devote to making them. So the majority of programme ideas come from within television. This is hardly surprising, since television attracts talented, creative people who have so much to offer in the way of ideas, and who are aware of the requirements and the limitations of television programme-making.

Even so, these ideas originate in a variety of ways. A producer might see a play in the theatre and decide to make it into a television drama. A writer might read a novel and feel that it would be suitable for converting into a television serial: *Treasure Island*, *Black Beauty* and *Tinker Tailor Soldier Spy* are well known examples of novels which have become successful television serials. The popular series *Coronation Street* started life over twenty years ago as a single play sent to the drama department by a hopeful playwright working in another part of that company. Humorous series like *Steptoe and Son* also developed from a single play, while others started as the germ of an idea in the mind of a producer, and were converted later into a series by professional script writers.

Television drama departments are always on the look-out for new plays and up-and-coming writers. Although many hopeful playwrights are disappointed by their early failure to break into the 'big time' of television, if there is real talent there it usually gets rewarded in the end.

Ideas for documentary programmes, too, come from various directions. It might be that a producer is curious about some aspect of life and feels that other people (namely the viewer at home) might be equally interested in seeing a programme devoted to that subject. People are basically curious, and almost any aspect of life can form the subject of a documentary. Sometimes someone is disturbed by something he has read or has heard, investigates further and emerges with a documentary programme which shocks people into sitting up, taking notice and sometimes doing something about a social disgrace. *Johnny*

The scene that has become so familiar over the years – Coronation Street.

Go Home and *Rampton, The Secret Hospital*, are two typical examples of this type of programme-making, brilliantly perfected by the award-winning producer, John Willis.

The lives of famous people are often fascinating and are a steady source of programme inspiration. Talking of famous people, television documentaries are often built around the special talents of brilliant reporters and personalities, who can choose the subjects they wish to explore because of their reputation and style. David Frost, Jonathan Dimbleby, and Robert Kee are excellent examples, and for twenty years or so Alan Whicker has wandered around the world and into our living rooms with his individual style of television reporting both for the BBC and Independent Television.

Documentary series, which are a number of programmes based on a single main theme, emerge when the subject is too vast to be covered in a single programme, and the popularity of *Hong Kong Beat*, *Arthur C. Clarke's Mysterious World*, *Sailor* and *Strangeways* surely justified the time and expense devoted to the making of them.

Sports action programmes happen, more often than not, because there is a sporting event which television sports producers know the viewers will want to see. The F.A. Cup Final, Wimbledon tennis, cricket test matches and rugby union internationals are very obvious examples of these types of programmes, and it does not require much genius on anyone's part to predict the success of television coverage of these events. Television has also played its part in popularising comparatively neglected sports, usually through the inspired vision of talented programme-makers and the courage of a television company to back their judgement. It was BBC television in its early days, which brought show jumping into the homes of millions of viewers who barely knew that it existed as a sport. Its popularity is still as strong today.

More recently, television has helped darts elevate itself from a game played and watched mainly in pubs and clubs into the highly commercialised spectacle we have become accustomed to. As a result, an elite group of superstars has emerged, travelling the world, playing tournaments for big money prizes and receiving payment from manufacturers of the goods they wear and the equipment they use. When not playing in tournaments they spend most evenings playing exhibition matches up and down the country, again for large fees. These players are immensely skilful, but they were known to comparatively few people until television took an interest in darts. Look, also, at what television has done for the sport of snooker, now one of the most popular of televised sporting events, thanks to the foresight of those who initially decided to go ahead with a programme called *Pot Black*.

In the world of light entertainment, of course, it is common for single shows and series to be fashioned around the talents of top entertainers: Morecambe and Wise, Harry Secombe, Shirley Bassey, Val Doonican and dozens more are now familiar to most viewers.

Because of the specialised requirements of television programme-making, then, the bulk of ideas for programmes come from the staff employed in a specific area. They know what it is and is not possible to do in any given time. They are well versed in what programmes the department has already covered and where it is looking for fresh suggestions. They know how to utilise every minute of valuable studio, film or outside broadcast time allocated to them, and do not put forward suggestions that are impossible to implement or too costly to contemplate. They know, too, the special guidelines or limitations laid down by governing bodies on what they may or may not do when making programmes in certain areas of television production. We have already mentioned the fact that religious programmes are carefully vetted by a committee set up for that purpose.

There are strict rules, too, about the content of children's programmes, but there is still a great variety throughout the range of children's television for ideas, good ideas, to flourish. Just think of the contrast between *Playschool*, *Grange Hill*, *Just William*, and *Blue Peter* and it is clear how much demand there is for all manner of ideas to provide programmes of interest for children of all age-groups, from the toddler stage upwards.

In the area of news and current affairs, the programme-makers are continually trying to keep abreast (even ahead) of the news. Some programmes are thrust on them, like the coverage of general elections. Regular news bulletins and daily regional news magazine programmes take up much of their time and consume vast quantities of material. Viewers these days have come to expect pictures from anywhere in the world showing events of interest within hours of their happening; sooner if possible. The next day other stories 'break', the interest shifts to another part of the world and the efforts of the previous day are forgotten, for, as the people who work on these type of programmes know, 'there is nothing as stale as yesterday's news'.

Then there are the 'in depth' type of current affairs programmes like *Panorama* and *Weekend World*, and the documentary-style *World in Action*, and *TV Eye*, which are dependent for their success not only on the inspiration but also the *news sense* of the production team. A good story and inspired presentation; with those two ingredients a current affairs programme is off the ground.

So the motivation for television programmes comes from a variety of directions. Many ideas are rejected or shelved for another day, but most end up as programmes for, as is becoming evident, television has a vast appetite. Once it is decided to make a programme and the date for transmission has been allocated, the programme-maker has a deadline to meet, and it is the ability to make good programmes within a specified time which is the hallmark of the professional. In the news and current affairs area it is not unknown for a major network programme to be suggested, made and transmitted in one day because of importance of a sudden happening. Usually, however, there is some time to prepare, and the care which goes into this is vital to the success of the making of the programme.

3 GETTING DOWN TO DETAIL

In order to understand the amount of preparation needed to produce a major television programme, it might help if we look at the thinking which must go into the planning of the most simple of shows.

Imagine a five-minute programme, transmitted late at night, just before the television transmissions for that evening come to an end, in which two people sit and talk to each other on a particular subject. Nothing could be simpler. Yet consider the decisions the programme-maker must make. The people are to sit facing each other – fine; but in what kind of chairs? Comfortable easy-chairs, contemporary leather, chrome, wooden or ... what? Should the chairs swivel or be fixed? What colour should they be? Would it be a good idea to place a table between them, and if so, what kind – solid wood, glass topped, round or square? Is there a need for anything on the table? A carafe of water and some glasses. Very well, which style of table-ware from the dozens available ... and why? Should there be a carpet on the floor (what type)? or should the floor be painted? If so, what colour, and why?

In what kind of 'set' should the people be placed? Not against a bare brick wall, surely. All right! Perhaps they should sit in front of some drapes, or a stretched backcloth. Certainly, but what colour and why? What of the overall lighting effect? Does it need to be bright and cheerful, or 'low key' and serious? What are the two people to wear? Sober suits, kaftans, or slacks and sports shirts ... and what colours?

Let us consider how we should start the programme. With a little music and some captions stating the name of the programme, a subtitle revealing the subject to be discussed, and the names of the two people involved? Good! But *which* bit of music would be appropriate for the programme and its subject matter? What are the people to talk about? Someone must decide on a subject and how it should be discussed. Will it take the form of a cosy chat, or a heated debate? Which of the two is to take the initiative, and come to that, who should the two participants be, and why? Should their discussion be illustrated, and if so with what – slides, film, video tape?

What should the programme be called? What of the lettering? There are hundreds of different styles to choose from, and the style chosen ought to match the mood of the programme. Let us not forget about colours. What colours should the lettering be and on what colour background? How should we end the programme? By lowering the lights, fading in the music and superimposing the 'end credits', as we call them? Or should one of the talkers turn to a camera and say 'goodnight'?

We have not even discussed the number of cameras to be used to 'shoot' the programme, nor where they should be placed in the studio to get the best shots, nor how these shots should be varied to provide interest, to show the attention of the listener, the sincerity of the speaker. We must be able to hear these artistes as they chat to each other on our screens. So they will need to be provided with microphones. Should these be attached to floor stands and pointed at the artistes for best results, or would that be unappealing to look at? Perhaps it would be better to use those tiny microphones fixed to the clothing of the speakers ('neck mics', as they are called) which are so unobtrusive but which unfortunately pick up the rustle of the clothing if the artiste fidgets constantly or plays nervously with his tie.

So that apparently simple programme is not so simple after all. It does not matter that it is a five-minute chat late at night, perhaps watched by very few people. If it is a programme to be transmitted it must be treated with professional respect, and all the points mentioned must be considered. Of course, the more experienced the programme-maker, the faster he will answer all those questions and the more sure he will be that his decisions will be the right ones, for that is what he is paid for – to be right.

Imagine, then, the decisions to be made by the person planning a television drama production. His programme will certainly involve more than one artiste, and they will probably spend some of the time moving around. The action, too, will take place in more than one setting – a kitchen, perhaps, a living room, the exterior and interior of a school, and so on.

Obviously there are many, many more decisions facing this programme-maker than with the simple programme we have just looked at. For a start, artistes have to be chosen, rehearsed, and the best performances encouraged from them. Since this is to be a television programme, the decisions as to how it will be shot have still to be made: the number and positions of the cameras; the relationship between the movement of artistes and cameras; the placing of microphones; the lighting effects; the use of music . . . the list seems endless.

That is work enough for anyone planning a single play. How much more there is to think of when engaged in a regular series of drama productions like *Coronation Street*, *Emmerdale Farm* and *Crossroads*. Each episode must receive the same thought, planning and care in production, week after week, year after year, if the illusion of reality is to be maintained in the eye of the viewer.

It is a credit to the programme-makers' skills that many viewers almost believe in the cameo of life presented to them and become involved in the 'lives' of the characters on the screen. Yet they are really make-believe programmes which exist firstly as a script, and then are shot and edited onto video tape by the programme-makers utilising the skills of very many people.

Let us look, then, at how a major drama series is produced week by week, and at the people involved in its making. Yorkshire Television's *Emmerdale Farm* is a good example for our purposes. In a typical year it appears on our screens twice a week for thirty-eight weeks. It is shot partly in the studio and partly by an outside broadcast unit on location, and planning, rehearsing, performing, recording and editing these seventy-six episodes during the year is a mammoth undertaking.

Emmerdale Farm, as its title suggests, is a continuing day-by-day account of the fictionalised lives of a rural community based around a typical Yorkshire farm. The programme reflects the real-life changes, problems, successes and failures of farming, and the human relationships in the tight community of village life. At the farm itself the home life revolves around the strong character of Annie Sugden, played by Sheila Mercier; but the series abounds in characters like Sam Pearson (Toke Townley), the pub landlord Amos (Ronald Magill), Seth Armstrong (Stan Richards), and the Reverend Donald Hinton (Hugh Manning).

Although the series has not been running as long as Granada's *Coronation Street*, it can look back over more than a decade of growing popularity, and the characters are now familiar to millions of viewers who would never miss an episode. Always the storylines attempt to keep pace with the fluctuations of modern farming, and the developments which are constantly introduced in real life. How to interweave these family and community conflicts within this farming environment, developing characters and maintaining dramatic appeal for month after month, is something we shall touch on later.

It must be added that there is a tremendous work-load on the artistes engaged in the series. A typical *Emmerdale Farm* script for just one episode is over forty pages thick, and that means a lot of learning to do for the actors and actresses, lines and lines of dialogue and acting instructions to be assimilated. As one batch of episodes is completed they move on to the next with its fresh new production team and director, as we shall see. For the artistes, however, it is business as usual; more lines, more action, more performances for the camera.

As in the film business, scenes are shot out of sequence, for many reasons, which presents its own problems for the cast. They are, in fact, an extremely professional group of artistes who can be relied upon at the end of the day to *deliver*. Whatever the delays and rescheduling, however the scenes are jumbled about to meet the demands of television shooting, month after month, year after year, they deliver the goods.

While the current series of episodes of *Emmerdale Farm* is under production and being recorded and transmitted, work starts six months in advance on planning the following year's production. At this early stage it involves four rather important people – the producer, the executive producer, the script editor and the series creator.

THE PRODUCER

In order to explain the producer's function we need to look first at someone else. As we shall see in greater detail later, the person responsible for taking the script of an episode and making a television programme from it is the director. He has at his disposal the crew and the artistes, and it is his function to direct the skills and talents of these people to provide a finished programme which will represent *his* interpretation of the written script.

As can be expected, not all directors work in the same way to achieve this. Their artistic and technical abilities differ, and they convert scripts into programmes in their own particular style.

Because of the demands of directing and the sheer volume of work involved, it is unrealistic to expect one director to supply all the episodes for a year's viewing, and so the work must be shared. Each television company has its own methods of spreading the work-load. At Yorkshire Television, six episodes of *Emmerdale Farm* are completed every four weeks. One director leading his production team is allocated for each batch of six episodes. In order to produce seventy-six episodes, in fact, ten different directors will produce six episodes each, with a further two directors producing eight each.

There are twelve production teams, then, under the control of twelve different directors. There is the danger that one batch of six episodes might look different in style from the next. So it is important that someone is responsible for ensuring that no matter which director is engaged in making a batch of six episodes for the series, the style of the programme, the standard of performance from the artistes, and the continuous flow of professionally competent programmes will be maintained. The person who does that is the producer, and on *Emmerdale Farm* his duties are extremely demanding and extend far beyond those mentioned.

He is responsible in the first place for planning the whole year's productions in advance. Every day that the studio will be needed must be calculated and booked, outside broadcast dates finalised, directors engaged, artistes contracted, writers commissioned: quite a task, as we shall see. In addition he holds the purse. Making television programmes is expensive, and unless someone keeps a tight rein on spending a series could price itself off the air. He is responsible, in fact, for the everyday running of the operation, which means that every detail which has to be attended to in the making of each episode is his concern. He does not attend to them himself, of course; that is what directors and others are there for. It is his concern nevertheless.

When all his careful plans for the months to come are disrupted by an industrial dispute, the sickness of a leading actor, the serious breakdown of equipment or inclement weather, it is he who must work out how to overcome these obstacles and get the production line flowing again as soon as possible. Keeping this production line flowing is one of the biggest headaches for the producer, for there can be major knock-on effects if one batch of six episodes is seriously delayed for any reason. Every effort is made to complete the four-weekly target on time so as not to interfere with the next six episodes scheduled for shooting over the following four weeks.

The weather in winter can be a particular problem. Not only can it disrupt attempts to maintain continuity from episode to episode, but it can be so intrusive as to cause story-lines to be diverted. Small falls of snow can be coped with and disguised by covering comparatively small areas with turf and shooting scenes in close-up. The furious snowstorms which are not unknown in North Yorkshire, however, can be a nightmare for everyone. Outside broadcast vehicles cannot get to locations or be moved to new ones. It is often impossible to change the story-line to include snow scenes because of previously shot and transmitted episodes. There is a limit to the number of interiors which can be recorded while waiting for the weather to clear, which can take weeks.

As valuable recording days slip away and the problems mount for *Emmerdale Farm*, the man with the responsibility for bringing the shooting schedule back on course as soon as possible is the producer.

Emmerdale Farm*'s well-known opening picture.*

Despite all his efforts it does happen occasionally that the six episodes cannot be completed within their scheduled four weeks. In that case the missing scenes must be shot during the next shooting period in addition to those already planned.

There is a gap of only two or three weeks between the completion of a batch of six episodes and the transmission of the first of them. So there is concern all round if more shooting has still to be done beyond the four weeks allocated. Sometimes other productions within Yorkshire Television must make way for the demands of *Emmerdale Farm*, so relentless is the pressure on the series to transmit its two episodes a week as scheduled and as advertised. Producer of *Emmerdale Farm* is no job for the lazy or those with weak nerves.

THE EXECUTIVE PRODUCER

Above the producer there is someone he can refer to at all times and to whom he is responsible, the executive producer. This figure may not get involved in the day-to-day planning and execution of the operation of getting *Emmerdale Farm* on the air twice a week, but he has the overall responsibility for ensuring that it gets there. He keeps an objective view of the production, then, and he has the final say on anything affecting the programmes. The producer is in constant, daily touch with him and although it is the producer's responsibility to attend to the details of keeping the operation running smoothly, the knowledge and approval of the executive producer is required for any deviations from the norm.

He also keeps an eye on the producer to see that *his* standards are not falling, or alternatively that he is not taking too much on himself at times of crisis and to get him help if it is needed.

THE SCRIPT EDITOR

In the same way that the producer ensures that the style of *Emmerdale Farm* episodes remains the same whoever is directing, a person known as the script editor keeps a tight control over the storylines, the style of writing and the quality of the work of the writers. A number of writers are commissioned each year to produce the scripts for the episodes of *Emmerdale Farm*, for the volume of work is too much for one man. Before any writer can put a sheet of paper in his typewriter and start work on a script, however, the script editor must give him guidelines to work to, a firm indication of how the lives of the characters will develop over the year ahead, the main plots and sub-plots, the peaks and troughs of life for the people of *Emmerdale Farm*.

THE SERIES CREATOR

What is known as the 'thrust of the storyline', then, is decided at that meeting six months before work starts on the following year's production, attended by the three people we have mentioned plus the man who originated the idea, the series creator, Kevin Laffan, who still writes episodes for the programme.

Over the next few weeks, these broad outlines are discussed in more detail, and with eighteen weeks to go the script editor is in a position to commission a writer to write six episodes. They meet, and the writer is told how the serial should progress through the six episodes, the storyline running through them, and the broad effect this will have on the characters. A couple of weeks later the writer submits his suggested storyline for the episodes he is responsible for, and if given the go-ahead he gets down to the actual business of writing the scripts.

He sends these to the script editor in batches of two, and with ten weeks to go to production the six episodes will all have arrived for scrutiny by the script editor and producer. If the writer is off course he is advised where he has gone wrong with his storyline and the way his characters are behaving. He then goes back to his typewriter and gets his episodes back onto course. Eventually, five weeks before production starts, all six scripts are approved, typed and distributed to the director and his production team.

It can be seen that getting the scripts together for just *one* batch of six episodes is a carefully controlled procedure, and there is no room for writers or script editors who 'put things off until tomorrow'. *Emmerdale Farm*, however, needs not six but seventy-six episodes to keep it going for a year. So, four weeks after the first writer has been commissioned to start work on his scripts, a second writer is commissioned for *his* batch of six episodes, and four weeks later a third writer starts work on *his* six; a never-ending, overlapping, avalanche of scripts to be written, discussed, rewritten, typed and distributed.

At last the scripts for six episodes are ready. The studio and outside broadcast dates are booked, the artistes contracted; now it is time to hand the process of making the six programmes over to the production team.

4 ENTER THE PRODUCTION TEAM

As we said earlier it is the director who has the responsibility for making six episodes in four weeks from the scripts handed to him by the producer. He has about a month in which to prepare for this, and so he gathers round him from the start the main members of his production team – his production assistant (PA), unit manager, designer, lighting director and stage manager.

THE PRODUCTION ASSISTANT

The PA is the director's right-hand woman. She is a person of many skills and she has a wide range of responsibilities. To many people from outside the television industry who come into contact with her, she seems to have a glamorous job – working alongside the director, often travelling around the world with him, and dealing at first hand with the famous people of showbiz, the theatre, the sporting world and so on.

There is no doubt that hers can be an exciting life at times. The work is varied, much depends on her efficiency and in many cases her personality, and there is a certain thrill in being in the forefront of television production. Nevertheless, on many programmes she is one of the hardest working members of the team. When with the director in his office she is rather like a personal secretary to a busy boss: typing correspondence, arranging appointments, attending to the routine paperwork of office life. If the director plans to go abroad for a couple of weeks to film a documentary, for example, she has the massive task of arranging flights, hotels, hire cars, foreign money and visas for everyone going on the trip, including the film crew of half-a-dozen people or more. Medical examinations must be organised, inoculations and vaccinations arranged and the schedule laying out the details of the two weeks' filming typed and distributed. Once abroad, or on location anywhere, in fact, she must keep a record of every detail of the shooting taking place, often typing this information in her hotel room long into the evening after a day's busy filming. She is constantly rearranging flights to meet new plans, re-booking hotel rooms and acting as nurse and mother to the rest of the crew.

Productions like *Emmerdale Farm*, which are shot partly in the studio and partly on location, give her other responsibilities: typing the camera script, for instance, in the way the director wishes it to be laid out; booking dressing rooms, arranging rehearsals, preparing the paperwork which ensures that those who should be paid for performing or assisting do get paid; there is so much she attends to.

Since there are only two PAs on *Emmerdale Farm* and twelve directors, these PAs move from a four-week stint with one director onto another four-week attachment with another. Their duties embrace a wide range of responsibilities. They must check and organise so many items before the commencement of a new shoot of four weeks to record six episodes that over the years a check-list has been built up. This details not only those which a new PA joining the series must attend to, but acts as a constant reminder (even to those familiar with the programme) of over fifty vital matters which cannot be left to chance.

The list runs to two-and-a-half foolscap pages as laid out below:

EMMERDALE FARM CHECK LIST

1. Check studio schedule and get production schedule.
2. Check editing dates and times (booked by producer) – memo to facilities department.
3. Check existence and tape number of opening titles.
4. Mark out timing sheet and do initial timing of episodes. Timings to Director/Script Editor.
5. Amend draft scripts as required and send off to Duplicating as rehearsal scripts (new front page).
6. Check character list on rehearsal script and type X-plot, specifying Outside Broadcast and Studio involvement.
7. Check internal distribution of rehearsal scripts done by Producer's Office – also scripts given out to Regulars. *All* cast to receive a full set of scripts.
8. Re-time rehearsal scripts as required.
9. Order any special facilities *in writing*.

⋆ ⋆ ⋆

16. Get new cast details as soon as possible – names, addresses, 'phone numbers – and check subsistence agreed.
17. Subsistence memo – regulars and non-regulars. Send memo to Artistes Payments.
18. Send rehearsal scripts (full set) to new cast + hotel list and letter giving first call (rehearsal or outside broadcast).
19. Inform Make-up and Costume of any new cast.
20. Check contracts for promised episodes, dates, etc. to tie in with X-plot and recording dates.
21. Ring new cast to check scripts received, correct spelling of name for credits, accommodation required and answer any queries.
22. Distribute full Artistes name and address list to Costume/Make-up/Floor Manager/Stage Manager/Producer's Office/Spares for Unit Assistants.
23. Send cast list to all cast.
24. End credits list – type and give to Producer for approval.

⋆ ⋆ ⋆

29. Book Dressing Rooms for Studio (none usually required for outside broadcast). See previous lists for usual plan.

30. Order outside broadcast tapes by memo (4 × 90 minute tapes for each week – 2 will probably be used and 2 available as spares).
31. Outside broadcast and Rehearsal Schedules – to Producer for approval. Distribution includes sets for artistes. Extra copies of outside broadcast schedules for outside broadcast survey.

★ ★ ★

36. Front page for camera script.
37. Camera script and camera cards.
38. Work out studio progress.
39. Check with Stills the day before a studio to check if there is to be a photocall.

★ ★ ★

42. Order tapes for editing.
43. Prepare editing notes.
44. Upgrading and fitting fees.
45. Get Sony tapes from Producer's Secretary and order copies to be made after editing. Memo to facilities.

★ ★ ★

49. Running time – minimum is 23.30 and maximum is 24.45.

ADDITIONAL NOTES

1. Script Editor
   Script editor and director will get together to amend the draft scripts. You type the amended pages, new front page and any changes to the running order. Script editor gets an update on the timings at the end of each week of production.

2. Camera Scripts
   All camera scripts contain a cast list and a set of synopses (to be provided by script editor).
   a) Outside broadcast scripts – front page, cast list, contact list, maps and directions, and then each day's call sheet + the script pages for that day. Each day is printed in a different colour.
   b) Studio scripts – front page, cast list, running order, synopses, scripts pages, closing caption lists.

And so it goes on.

Perhaps much of that will be gibberish to most readers, but it illustrates the attention to detail that is inseparable from non-stop productions of this nature. The PA is not just a girl with a stopwatch, a clipboard and a swagger. She is a hard-working and vital member of a professional television production team who carries a great deal of the responsibility for keeping the treadmill revolving.

She sits alongside the director in the control room, or the mobile control room if she is at an outside broadcast, timing each scene as it is shot, noting the number of times a scene is recorded (the number of 'takes' as we call them) and any comments the director might make about each. Her function while scenes are being recorded is to 'log' everything which happens and the time at which they did. Later, when scenes have to be found on video tape for editing purposes, her notes will be invaluable. The timings she made weeks before were also electronically recorded onto the video tape, and it becomes a simple matter to spin through that tape to find any scene required.

On other types of programmes, as we shall see later, the PA can be extremely busy in a totally different way, especially on those programmes which are transmitted 'live' as they happen. In addition, there is so much more to the PA's work that is often forgotten, even by members of her own production team: the amount of typing and retyping, for instance, as scripts are amended and improved; the long hours into the evenings, and sometimes the night, to meet deadlines that will not wait; the days when it seems that no-one appears to notice her efforts until something is not right, when the blame, sometimes unfairly, is levelled at her.

Some PAs work with one director over many years, others work in a particular department and are allocated to whichever director is engaged. As we now know, *Emmerdale Farm* relies on two PAs who alternate on each block of six episodes.

The PA is a very important member of the production team, therefore. Although the job might not be as glamorous as it first appears, it is still one of the most rewarding jobs in television for the intelligent, hard-working and efficient woman. She must be a fast and accurate typist; strangely, shorthand is rarely required. She must be forceful, inventive, reliable, and tireless. She cannot be a clock-watcher and still do her job effectively, and it follows that mistakes and laxity on her part can have a demoralising and destructive effect on productions in which she is involved.

THE UNIT MANAGER

Not every television company uses a unit manager, which is surprising since he is extremely useful to have on the team. In simple terms, his responsibility is the smooth-running of the production the director is engaged on. He is really at his busiest on location work, both on filming and outside broadcast assignments. Co-ordinating the efforts of four dozen people spread over an acre of land in the vicinity of a farm, each engaged on his own particular task, is no easy matter. He has radio contact with the director sitting in his mobile control room (or 'scanner' as it is usually called). Since this scanner might be a half-a-mile or more from the action taking place, the director is totally reliant on the unit manager to pass on his instructions to whoever they are meant for.

He must be very organised himself, preparing for the next scene whilst still engaged on the one being recorded, for much time can be lost moving people and equipment from one site on a location to another. Good planning and organisation on his part can minimise this. An interesting side to his work is finding new locations. The script might contain a scene involving a cottage under a steep, vertical cliff, a boathouse on an island in a river, or a farm on the edge of a forestry site. It is the unit manager who must find these, and since *Emmerdale Farm* prefers locations no further than about 18 miles from the studios in Leeds (to keep down the time-wasting travelling involved and costs) his task is not always easy.

Nevertheless he will come up with just the right site more often than not. One unit manager working on another major drama series, but with the same limitations regarding distance, was asked to find sites resembling a peninsula in the Russian steppes, a typical street in Brussels, the exterior and interior of a hotel in Sri Lanka, and some typical Cyprus countryside. He found them all within 20 miles of a large English industrial town.

When the programme moves into the television studio, the unit manager's duties are similar to those on location work, but his title now changes to floor manager. He is responsible for studio discipline, for passing on instructions to artistes, for co-ordinating the efforts of such people as stage hands, the property department, make-up, wardrobe and many more we shall be meeting later. The director talks via a microphone to the cameramen on the studio floor because they wear headphones ('cans' as we call them), as well as to some other technicians and, of course, to the floor manager. It is the floor manager's job, then, to pass on the director's instructions to anyone not wearing 'cans'.

A good unit/floor manager is invaluable. He can save the most precious of commodities during the shooting of a programme – *time*. If a director wants to start recording a scene at 3 pm, he is entitled to expect that the artistes will be standing by, properly dressed and made-up, with the crew ready to start, and everything and everyone in their places. It is the unit manager's responsibility to make sure this happens. Ten minutes wasted while someone changes into a pair of gumboots which he left in his dressing room, and five minutes wasted at the start of another recording soon add up to hours during four weeks of shooting. That sort of thing does not happen when a good unit manager is in charge.

We mentioned earlier the PA's responsibilities on locations, particularly overseas assignments. These usually apply to documentary-type filming, of which more later. Apart from factual programmes of that nature, it is the unit manager who attends to all the large and small details which enable a production, in particular a drama production or series, to function efficiently without the irritating delays which can throw the best-organised of schedules into disarray.

As in the case of the PA it is assumed that the unit manager is tireless. The director relies on his constant attention to every instruction throughout long and busy days. The unit manager, as we have seen, is

A designer working on a model of a set.

often the director's only link on location between the scanner and the artistes. He must be firm yet tactful. He must have initiative and drive. He is expected to think of everything which needs to be done to keep the production running smoothly. He also cannot be a clock-watcher. He must give himself, his efforts, and his time to his programme. There is no other way to do the job well.

THE DESIGNER

Probably no-one helps the director to portray the illusion of reality on the screen more than the designer. It is he who has the task of creating totally believable sets from wood and plaster, paint and glue. He must be very artistic, have a keen eye for detail, and be aware of the specialised requirements of television production, lighting and camerawork. Yet he must be practical, for no matter how wonderful his sets might be they are no use to the director if they take two years to make, need a crane and fifty workers to get them into the studio, and cost a million pounds.

Television studios do not have elastic walls, and the designer is expected to be a genius at cramming the required number of sets into a studio, yet still leaving enough room for all the equipment needed to shoot a television programme. *Emmerdale Farm* usually records exterior scenes in the village chosen for the series, and at the farm which has become its permanent home. Most interior scenes are shot in the studio in Leeds using the sets created by the designer, and now so familiar to millions of viewers.

There was a time, of course, however, when those sets did not exist, so let us look at how they came into being. In the first place the director and the designer studied the script very carefully until they were satisfied as to which interiors they must create and how they should be arranged to accommodate the action which would take place in them. The next step was to visit the outside locations which these interiors must match. *Emmerdale Farm* uses three standard interiors around which the lives of the characters mainly revolve: the farmhouse, the pub and the vicarage. The designer studied the exteriors of these places at the locations chosen by the director, noting particularly the types of doors and windows used, and their positions. He took polaroid photographs and made many sketches to help him when back at his drawing-board he tried to design an authentic-looking interior to match the original.

He also made a careful note of the view from these locations, for he would have to paint a replica of this view onto a large 'back-cloth'. This would hang outside the window of the set when erected in the studio, adding to the feeling of authenticity. He then provided the director with drawings of these interiors as he imagined them. Once the director was satisfied with these, the designer then arranged them in plan form on a floor-plan of the studio. He also prepared detailed drawings to be sent to the people who would construct these sets. Later, as we shall see, someone will provide the bits and pieces, the furniture and personal possessions, which add to the illusion of reality. The set will be painted and decorated, too, exactly as the designer requires.

The viewers at home see only those parts of the set which the director instructs his cameramen to include in their shots, and the eye and brain are soon lulled into believing that they are seeing the actual interior of the farm, the pub, the vicarage. If we look at the set of the pub, for example, in the studio, this illusion soon disappears. For a start the 'room' has only three walls; one side will have been left open so that the cameras can point at the action taking place there. The set has no ceiling. Where the ceiling would normally be, dozens of lamps hang at different heights, apparently pointing in haphazard directions, flooding the room with light.

No matter how solid and firm the walls of the room might seem on the screen, they are in fact made of wood. As they stand on the studio floor they are held in position from behind by braces, which themselves are held firm by large metal weights, called stage-weights. All part of the make-believe world of television.

In fact there is nothing particularly magic about this kind of layout. Anyone who has been to the theatre or performed in amateur dramatics will be familiar with the three-sided set and the theatrical tricks

The designer's sketch of the kitchen set for Emmerdale Farm.

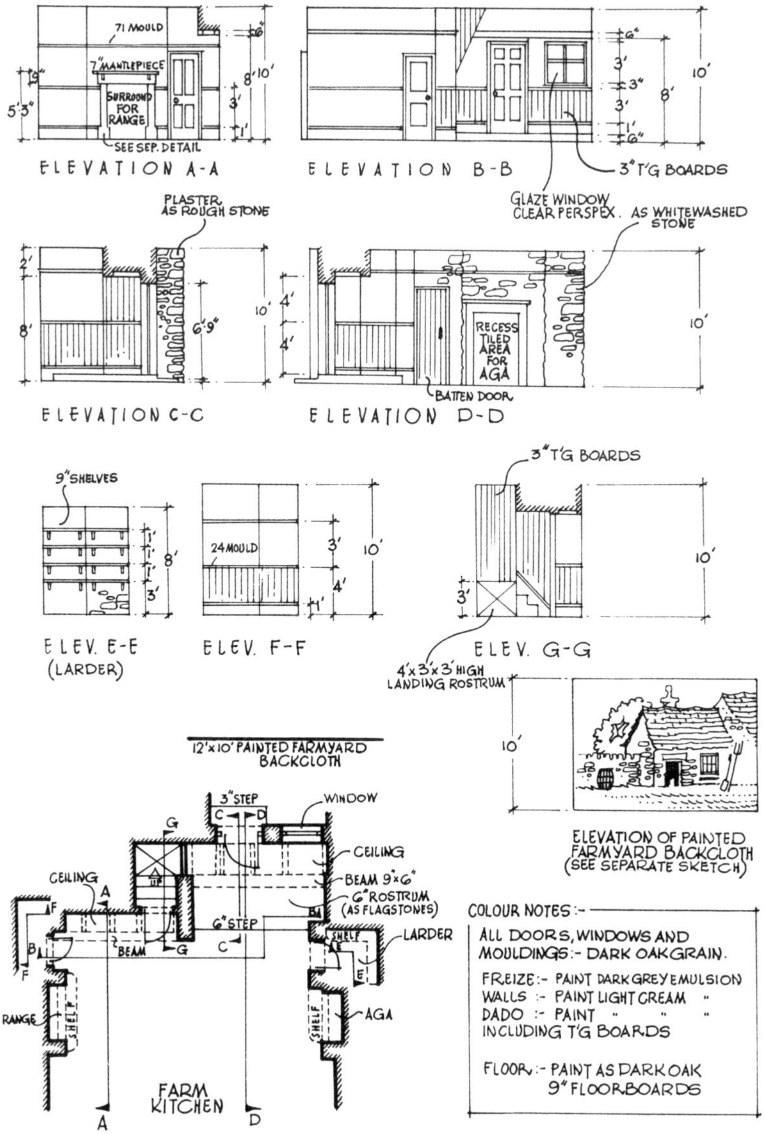

The designer's construction plan and working drawings for the kitchen set of Emmerdale Farm.

employed to lull the audience into thinking that they are looking at a slice of reality. There are differences, of course. The location of the various sets around the studio floor is governed by the requirements of television – access to cameras, sound and lighting. If a small scene is scripted to take place, say, at the foot of a flight of stairs, then only that portion of the staircase which will be embraced in the cameraman's shot is constructed and placed in the studio. Quite obviously there is no point in providing areas of sets which will never be seen.

Good designers are almost revered by directors in television for they always seem to improve on the director's concept of how the set should look. It is quite surprising how they create apparent reality from plans and drawings, wood and paint, furniture and props. Their attention to detail must be absolute. They are a rare combination of two apparently conflicting characteristics: artistic vision and down-to-earth practicality. They must be cost-conscious, space-conscious and time-conscious. Yet these considerations must not be allowed to cramp their creative expression. Above all they must deliver on time exactly what is required, a set which looks right for the programme and which is practical in terms of television coverage.

THE LIGHTING DIRECTOR

The designer cannot expect his sets to come to life without the co-operation of another skilled, artistic member of the team, the lighting director. In order to obtain television pictures from a camera, the subject the camera points at must have an adequate amount of light falling on it. In order to obtain good, artistic, dramatic pictures, it is important that the lamps directed at the subject be carefully arranged to give the effect required.

Take the simple example of a newscaster sitting at his desk in front of a painted wall of wood, called a 'flat', on which have been written the words 'News Desk'. He is sitting firmly in his chair, and there is just one camera pointing at him. Yet to produce a picture of the newscaster which looks as near to three-dimensional life as it is possible to get with a two-dimensional picture, four basic lights are needed. Pointing a bright light straight at him will produce a flat featureless face, no feeling of shape, and very little impression of what the person really looks like. The background, too, will probably be mainly in shadow, and the wording on the flat difficult to read.

This is where the lighting director comes into the picture, for it is his job to direct the lights at his disposal to help produce good, lifelike television pictures. Back to our newscaster, sitting patiently at his desk. The lighting director will point one light at the face from partly to one side to throw shadows from the nose and other features. A gentler light from the other side will soften those shadows. A third light will illuminate the flat and a fourth light will shine on the

The lighting director supervising the placing of every lamp needed.

newscaster's shoulders from behind to help separate him from the background in the viewer's eye.

Of course there is more to it than that, for the lighting director must decide how high each lamp must be suspended from the floor, the type of lamps used for each of those four functions, and the individual intensity of each lamp to get the best effect. That is enough technical talk for now. But it does help to illustrate the difficulties the lighting director faces when he has to light the action taking place in a set where there may be many artistes, much movement and a great variety of camera positions.

In addition to merely directing the lights to obtain good television pictures, the lighting director can do much to set the mood of a scene by his clever use of lighting techniques. By utilising modern computerised lighting consoles, which help govern which set of lamps are lit at any time to create the right effect, a touch of a button will transform a scene from day to night or from summer to winter.

He can work wonders with coloured lights, too, and it is worthwhile studying clever use of lighting during such programmes as musical spectaculars and televised plays when watching television at home.

THE STAGE MANAGER

The fifth member of the production team who helps the director in his search for the illusion of reality is the stage manager. (This job is

Props are arranged under the eye of the designer.

frequently done by women, so to avoid confusion with the unit/floor manager let us assume that our stage manager is a lady!) Her function is to provide those bits and pieces we mentioned earlier which add the final touches to the efforts of the designer to make his sets look authentic.

The designer is responsible overall for deciding how the set should be 'dressed' with furniture and props, and he uses a polaroid camera to record the final effect to help maintain continuity over the weeks and years to come. To go back to the sets of *Emmerdale Farm*, all those 'props' which make it look so believable will have come from the stage manager: bottles, glasses, ash trays, cloths, wall pictures, crockery, cutlery, vases, flowers and many, many more items. In fact, anything in the sets which people use, look at, eat or drink will be the stage manager's responsibility, although the men of 'props and scenes' will actually place them where needed.

It is worth looking at the responsibilities of the stage manager for they are not totally centred around the bits and pieces of television sets. The stage manager on *Emmerdale Farm* must learn as much as she can about the story's characters. Do they have their own mugs, or other items with which they feel familiar? Where do they sit when eating or relaxing? Which kitchen items does Annie Sugden use when baking? Understanding the character in the series enables the stage manager to provide the right items to help these characters to feel that the set is their home, as familiar and secure as if this is where they really spend their lives.

Keeping continuity among the props used in the programme is constantly on the stage manager's mind. Firstly, because scenes are not recorded in the order laid down by the storyline (which we shall look at later), the stage manager makes notes and takes photographs to ensure that whatever order the scenes are approached the right bits and pieces will be in the right place and in the right condition. Secondly, continuity is important when looking at a character's personal effects. If someone always uses a certain type of pipe, for example, it will disturb the artiste if presented with the wrong one. Any errors of this nature will certainly be noted by the viewers, who will write to complain in their hundreds.

Attention to detail, then, is one of the most important attributes a stage manager must possess, but it is very important that she has a 'feel' for the characters in the series and for the artistes portraying them. This is particularly useful when a new director arrives for his six-episode assignment, unfamiliar with the cast and the minute idiosyncracies of the characters.

When the stage manager receives her copies of the scripts for six episodes she first of all notes all those props needed in the order laid down by the story; the order in which they will be seen by the viewer when all the scenes have been shot and edited to produce the finished programmes. She has many discussions with the director and designer to confirm the exact nature of the props required. She prepares lists of those which have to be acquired, and meets with the property buyer who will get these for her. She approaches other departments for such items as cookers which have to work in the studio, sinks which have running water, gas supplies. As props arrive she checks them carefully.

She then notes the order in which scenes will be shot and prepares lists detailing the props needed for each scene *as it will be recorded*, giving as much information as possible to the studio hands about the action of the scene and the 'role' of the props (drawing maps and diagrams if needed) to help rehearsals and recordings run smoothly. Scenes in which the characters are eating can be quite a headache for her, for they are sometimes recorded many times before the director is satisfied, and each new recording will need a fresh meal laid out exactly as it was on the first take, and just as hot and appetising.

Because of the vast number of different scenes stage managers have been responsible for over the years, they can all tell of the remarkable things directors have asked them to find. A set of elephant's tusks, a life-support machine, a rickshaw, an American freeway sign, a gondola, six boomerangs, a cobra, a World War One aeroplane, four skeletons representing mother, father and two teenage children, and a partridge in a pear tree!

When all recording is completed she makes notes of any new continuity requirements which have emerged for any particular character or set, taking photographs if needed. These are necessary not only for her own reference, but for the benefit of any other stage managers who will follow her. The props are wheeled away in their cages, to be stored until the next six episodes get under way. 'Thank you' notes then follow to contacts, friends, colleagues and others who have helped provide the items needed.

So the director has gathered his team around him for the detailed preparations necessary to produce six episodes of *Emmerdale Farm* in four weeks . . . to 'get them in the can', as they say in television.

5 OVER TO YOU, MR DIRECTOR

The director has the scripts for each of his episodes, he has his production team, and the dates allocated to him for both OB (outside broadcast) and studio shooting. He plots the way he will record all the scenes for all six episodes very carefully, for time with the cameras and artistes is precious. He studies each script and divides the action to be covered into two main sections: those to be shot in the studio and those on OBs.

Taking the OB action, he notes each area where scenes must take place, and makes a list of what those scenes are and in which episodes they appear. Let us say that there are seven scenes to be recorded in the farmyard: one for episode one, one for episode three, two for episode five, and three for episode six. Then that is how the scenes will be shot. It is common sense, once cameras and other equipment have been manhandled into place, to record all the scenes needed there and then, before moving onto the next set-up. Of course, recording in this fashion can cause problems of continuity as we shall see later.

A shooting order, then, is issued to everyone concerned with the production, which obviously sets out the order in which scenes will be shot; quite different from the order in which they will appear in the finished programmes. Of course it is not quite as straightforward as that, for the scenes may have to take place at differing times of day, and this must be taken into account when planning the shooting. This is an example of part of the shooting order:

Episode	*Scene*	*Location*	*Artistes*	*Notes*
990	3	Exterior farmyard	Annie/Sam	No dialogue
992	6	Exterior farmyard	Seth/Jack	Noon
992	11	Exterior farmyard	Seth/Annie	Dusk Sheep

The shooting order for every day follows this pattern, so that every scene to be shot is listed and earmarked for recording. Everyone on the unit knows when their contribution is required, therefore, and sets about preparing for this involvement in their own way. Studio shooting is planned in a similar manner. We have already seen how the stage manager sets about preparing her props, for example, so that all will be waiting in good time for the artistes, the 'scenes and props', and the director.

When preparing a shoot in this manner the director is in constant

Shooting Emmerdale Farm *on location.*

touch with the designer. Extra sets might be needed in the studio, for example, to complement some new exteriors which are included in the scripts. The designer issues studio floor-plans showing the layout of all sets to be erected in the studio and the director details the location of cameras and other equipment which will cover the action within them. These plans are needed not only by the men who will place these sets in the studio exactly where required, but also by the lighting director who must plot and supervise the rigging of every lamp which will be needed to light the sets correctly and artistically for television. The lighting director is often needed on OB locations, too, compensating for poor natural light, for example, or softening the hard shadows thrown by strong sunlight. OBs are not all confined to exterior scenes, either.

Of course, the unit manager is not idle. He is in constant touch with the director, noting everything he must attend to if the operation is to run smoothly. The PA issues what is termed a 'call sheet' which lists, in great detail, the production team's every requirement for the days in the studio. The unit manager issues the call sheet for the OB locations, and nothing is left to chance. This is an example of a section of such a call sheet to set up an OB location to shoot just seven scenes in and around a pub. This gives some idea of the amount of preparation and planning which must go into the *six episodes* the production team must shoot.

ARTISTES' CALLS:

Artistes	*Characters*		*at studio*	*Costume/M.UpReq. on location*	*on set*
Arthur Pentelow	Wilks	at home	0830	0900	0930
Peter Schofield	Ernie		0800	0900	0930
Sandra Gough	Doreen		0800	0900	0930
Toke Townley	Sam	at hotel	0915	0945	1015
Stan Richards	Seth		0900	0945	1015
Johnny Caesar	Bill		0900	0945	1015
Ronald Magill	Amos	at home	0900	0945	1015
Al Dixon	Walter	at home	0915	0945	1015
Extras: 13 male	6 female		0745		

OB TECHNICAL REQUIREMENTS:
as Wednesday
TRANSPORT REQUIREMENTS:
One 29-seater coach: To be at Studio at 0745 to collect Costume Make-up and 19 Extras and be on location at 0845.
HIRE CARS REQUIRED:
One taxi: To collect PETER SCHOFIELD and SANDRA GOUGH at Studio at 0800 then on to collect ARTHUR PENTELOW from his home at 0830 and be on location by 0900.
One taxi: to collect RONALD MAGILL from his home at 0900 then to collect TOKE TOWNLEY from his hotel at 0915 and to be on location by 0945.
One taxi: To collect JOHNNY CAESAR at Studio at 0900 and then collect AL DIXON from his home at 0915 and to be location at 0945.
Own transport: STAN RICHARDS.
CATERING:
Breakfast: 0845
Lunch: 1300–1400
Afternoon Break: To be arranged
Approx. numbers: 60
Dining coach: required.
PARKING:
OB VEHICLES, GENERATOR, CATERERS
Please park behind Pub as per plan.
PRIVATE VEHICLES:
As per plan.
NOT IN FRONT OR ON APPROACH TO PUB.
ARTISTES' CARAVANS:
ONE CARAVAN with heating, lighting and spare gas to be on location at 0830 and to park behind pub as per plan.
COSTUME & MAKE-UP:
COSTUME CARAVAN: To be on location at 0830 and park behind pub as per plan.
MAKE-UP: in small bar of Pub.
ACTION VEHICLES:
None
ANIMALS:
None

PROPS: As per Stage Manager's and Designer's lists.
PROP VAN: To deliver props by 0845.
ADDITIONAL REQUIREMENTS:
None

This is followed by extremely detailed routes to the location, sometimes with a separate set of instructions for those driving the scanner and other large vehicles where narrow roads or weak bridges make diversions necessary.

About two weeks before the artistes are due in the studio for a block of six episodes, they receive their rehearsal scripts so they can set about the all important business of learning the dialogue and understanding the storyline. They will spend two days in the studio (a Thursday and a Friday) and four days on OB to record the six episodes.

On the Friday afternoon before their first studio day, and then on the following Monday, Tuesday and Wednesday they assemble in a special rehearsal room within the Yorkshire Television complex. This modestly-sized room is where they rehearse their dialogue and action under the watchful eye of the director. In the room there is a mock-up of the bar of the 'Woolpack', *Emmerdale Farm*'s well-known pub. Other rooms are marked out on the floor with coloured tape by the stage manager so that the artistes are reminded of the boundaries within which they must work and the location of items of furniture. At these rehearsals, too, the director finalises the position his cameras will take in the studio on the Thursday and Friday recording days.

On the Tuesday morning of rehearsals the lighting director, sound supervisor and designer usually attend to finalise their preparations for the coming recordings. On Wednesday afternoon the rehearsal room is a little crowded as cameramen, make-up, wardrobe, vision mixer and sometimes the producer study the final rehearsal, and each marks his or her scripts with their own professional shorthand. The cast do not rehearse in this way for the OB scenes. These are normally rehearsed on site until the director is satisfied and then recorded.

ON LOCATION

At eight-o-clock on a raw, wintry, North Yorkshire morning the cluster of buildings and fields known to millions of viewers as *Emmerdale Farm* has nothing of the glamour which people often assume to be associated with making television programmes on location. A heavy frost, a stinging north-east wind and the promise of sleet to come, soon remind early arrivals that television is a job, and that creating make-believe often has the icy touch of reality about it.

Already the generator which supplies power to the OB unit is humming away, and a light flickers on in the make-up caravan as the two girls arrive and set out their equipment. Make-up girls insist that their job is not glamorous, despite the popular image to the contrary. They point out that it is always tiring, rarely comfortable,

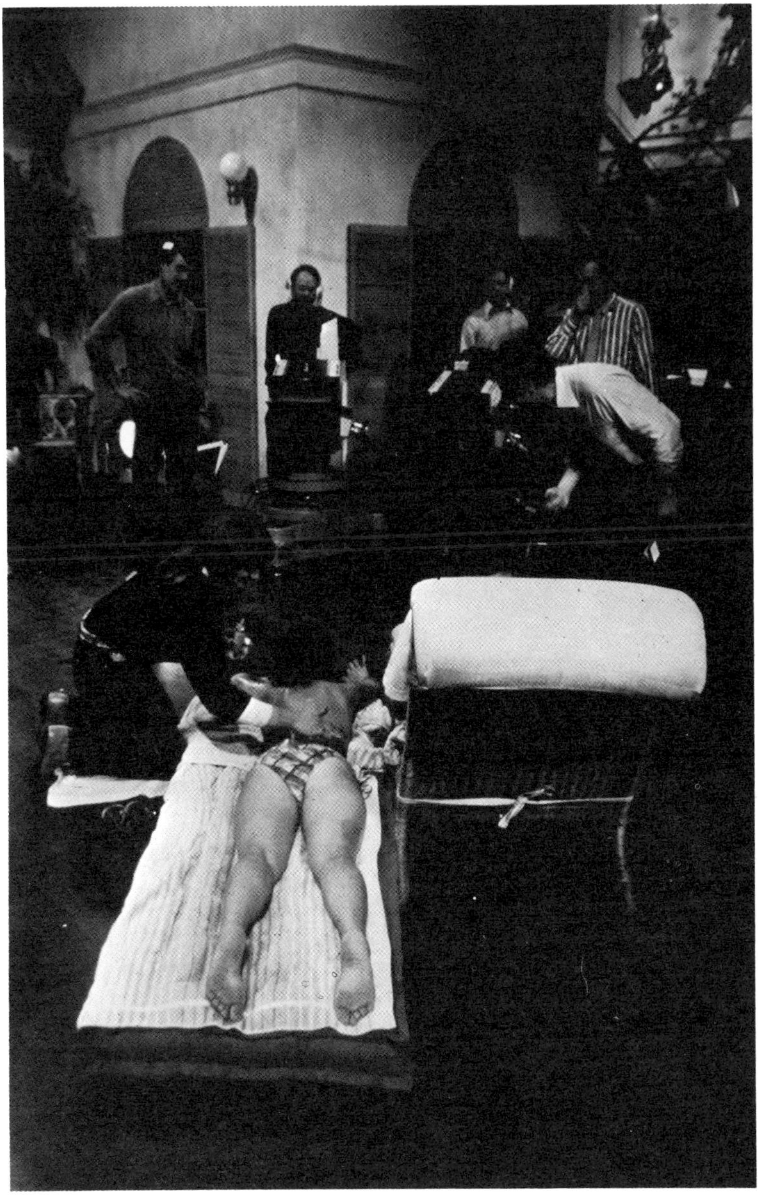

Make-up can be added where necessary at any time during shooting.

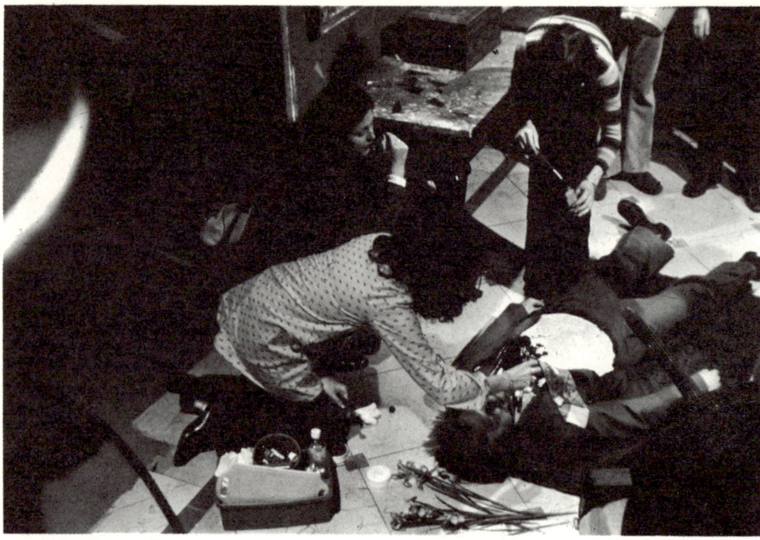

If they need blood, they make it....

and sometimes downright unpleasant. At 8 am on a February morn, who could argue? Their first task on arriving at the caravan is to plug in the heated rollers and brushes ready for the first of the artistes to arrive at around 8.30 am. Then they set out their equipment, towels, soaps, shavers, lotions, creams, powders and so on. The caravan is supplied with hot and cold running water, of course, and plenty of lighting, for make-up must be performed under the most searching of lights.

It takes them around half-an-hour on average to make up the female artistes; about half that time for the men. Specialised work, however, can take three hours or more, and if blood is needed – they make their own! There are fourteen main characters in the programme and over the years the make-up girls get to know them very well, with all the plusses and minuses which attend familiarity. The girls get to know the idiosyncrasies of each artiste and the requirements of the character he or she plays. Make-up girls are extremely discreet. They have to be, for not only do they see the weaknesses and flaws of the 'stars', but there are even more intimate exchanges of confidences between them than those traditionally made between the housewife and the hairdresser.

They are always expected to be cheerful, well groomed and tireless, and this, paradoxically, they find one of the most tiring aspects of their work. They would not be in the profession if they had a dislike of people, and they usually are to be found smiling, raising morale, and rebuilding confidence with their personality and make-up skills.

Emmerdale Farm is now a major tourist attraction. This is the artistes' eye view of location shooting.

Not all *Emmerdale Farm* locations are centred around the site of the farm itself, so when the OB unit moves on they gather their boxes of equipment and follow. At the new location there might be a caravan for them, perhaps the 'snug' of a pub, perhaps a room in a cottage borrowed for the day in which to carry on their work.

Having made up the artistes, their job is not over. They must be in attendance at each scene, tramping across fields and streams with the rest of the team, to check the make-up at the end of each 'take' and to repair and renew any 'damage'. They, too, must be aware of the need to maintain continuity, so they take polaroid pictures of any specialised make-up which must be repeated on another day at another location.

Creative they must be. Yet they must also be practical, resilient and not a little diplomatic. But in their caravan this freezing, February morning their thoughts are directed only at the day ahead. They will be on their feet much of the time, tending to their charges as they follow one another into the little hut. 'Could someone fetch us a coffee, please?'.

From the large catering van bacon, egg and sausage sandwiches, supplemented by coffee and tea, are eagerly clutched and carried to the large, heated, wooden canteen by the crew members. The field which acts as a car park rapidly fills as artistes and crew arrive. The car

A typical outside broadcast unit on location.

bringing Toke Townley from his Leeds hotel arrives and returns to collect Sheila Mercier who is not needed until 10 am.

In the huge costume van the wardrobe staff prepare for the day ahead. All the costumes used on location yesterday were taken back to the studios and washed that evening. Now they are clean and ironed; that was done at 7.30 this morning at the studios. Many viewers assume that the characters on *Emmerdale Farm* wear their own clothes, which is not the case. So in the same way that the stage manager prepares her props for the scenes to come, so the wardrobe staff make ready every item of clothing which will be needed for every scene to be shot.

By 9 am on the Sunday prior to a week's OB they must prepare a complete list of all costumes to be needed that coming week so that these can be loaded into their large van and transported to the OB location. Normally something like a hundred and fifty costumes are taken out to the location to cover the four days of shooting, and the attention to detail is as precise as one would expect from these committed professionals. For every scene to be shot, both on location and in the studio, the correct costume must be available for the character, and once again, because scenes are shot out of sequence, the staff must ensure that if Jack walks into the pub wearing a certain set of clothes (and shot in the studio) he is wearing the same set of clothes when he leaves the pub (when that scene is shot on location).

The costume staff make copious notes and take photographs to

The costume department preparing for a period drama.

prevent mistakes happening. There are over a thousand costumes in *Emmerdale Farm*'s wardrobe, and this is not surprising if we look at the facts. Apart from the fourteen main characters who need a wide range of costumes, not only for a variety of both indoor and outdoor circumstances but also to keep pace with the changing seasons, there must be provision for the characters who sometimes 'drop in' on the series, and also to allow for extras and emergencies.

To help keep track of all these costumes and to assist with continuity, they are all numbered and described on the costume sheets, which are prepared for every block of *Emmerdale Farm* shooting. In addition, there are so many shirts in use that each shirt belonging to each character receives its own number to avoid any confusion. The sheets are laid out as follows, and there are sixteen or more to cover just two day's studio recording.

Episode	*Scene*	*Day*	*Time*	*Synopsis of scene*	*Studio Thurs/Fri. Feb 18/19*
987	2	892	8.30 am	Back Room Woolpack *Breakfast* take picture (polaroid)	Amos. Costume 1. Brown trousers, blue sweater shirt. Slippers. Sleeves rolled up. Wilks. Costume 1. Cavalry twills, smoke shirt (No. 1), slippers (possibly apron). Sleeves rolled up to elbows.
990	3	894	11.15 am	Woolpack Bar	Amos. Costume 4. Blue trousers, green shirt, dark green cardigan. Slippers.
990	4	894	6.00 pm	Woolpack Bar	Walter. Costume 1.
					Outside Broadcast. Wed Feb 26
993	4	897	2.30 pm	Ext. field	Matt. Costume 1. Brown cords, black and yellow check shirt (No. 6), black fleck sweater, green boiler suit, wellies, thick socks, Parka Brown woolly hat.

Out on location the supervisor, his assistant and two dressers (one male and one female) attend to the needs of the cast. Contrary to what one might think, the dressers do not actually put the clothes on helpless artistes. Their function is to check that characters have the right clothes, to hang up discarded clothing and to lay out in advance the costume the artiste will require next.

Their first task on arriving at the location is to warm the clothes to be used first, partly because no-one likes putting on cold clothes on any icy morning, and partly because there will certainly have been some condensation during the night and the costumes are likely to be a little damp. Like the make-up girls, they too are at takes, ensuring continuity and attending to the costumes. There are two caravans used for changing, one each for male and female artistes and as they are not very big they can become rather crowded and claustrophobic, particularly when half-a-dozen men plus the dresser are all trying to get out of one rain-soaked set of clothes and into fresh outfits.

Muddy boots at the end of a day's recording present a problem, particularly if the character has emerged from a cow-shed! Tomorrow a scene might have to be shot with the same character wearing the same boots with the same pungent pattern of farm muck. The boots cannot be left in the costume van, if only because the smell would permeate the other clothing. In any case the mixture will cake and present a different sight the next day. There is no alternative but to take a polaroid photograph of the boots, hose them clean, and mess them up again the following day to match the photograph.

At the end of the day's shoot it is back to the studios for the wardrobe department. Costumes must be washed ready for ironing the next morning at 7.30. Long hours, then, and hard work are the lot of these people. Yet they like working on *Emmerdale Farm*. They know all the artistes and their likes and dislikes, unlike moving from single play to single play when they must get to know new people all the time. Three-quarters of costume staff are, not surprisingly, female, and it is a department which relies heavily on freelance staff who can be called on for comparatively short periods to cope with heavy work-loads. In fact around 50 per cent of dressers in television are recruited in this manner.

Meanwhile, as the costumes are hung on rails in the van, grouped in blocks under the names of the characters, back at the scanner (the mobile control room) there are signs of life. Technicians switch on equipment, warm up cameras, plug in microphones, and check signals and communications. In another van the video tape engineers load spools of tape onto their machines and go through the careful procedure of setting up their equipment for the recordings to come.

Two cameras are manhandled into a position at the edge of a field for the first scene, their cables winding back across the frosty field, through a hedge and into the side of the scanner. Dozens and dozens of cables spew out from the scanner's underbelly, obscenely, like entrails. Leaning against the make-up van the director goes through the day's shooting with the unit manager and PA. The two artistes for the first scene arrive dressed and made-up, and the director has a last chat with them before the unit manager takes them off to the first location.

The director climbs into the comparative warmth of the cramped, darkened scanner. Ahead of him a bank of monitors show him the pictures from each of his cameras. To one side of him sits the vision mixer, ready to cut from camera to camera on his instructions. To the other side sits the ever-present PA, her scripts, clipboard, stopwatches and other necessary items taking up much room on the narrow desk in front of her. Scene three of episode 990 is about to be rehearsed and recorded.

IN THE STUDIO

For only two days out of the concentrated four weeks needed to produce six episodes, the director has the use of a studio. Here the interior scenes are shot which must complement the OB exteriors. Two days is not a lot of time by any standards in which to gather all the interiors needed for the episodes under production.

The sets are taken into the studio and erected during Tuesday night, and are then dressed with props and furniture and lit by the lighting director throughout Wednesday. For three hours on Thursday morning and four-and-a-quarter hours in the afternoon (with time taken out for coffee breaks and other stoppages) scenes are rehearsed and recorded as per the running order. On Friday there is less time, a total of six hours, so the behind-the-scenes activity is stepped up.

The preparation, as ever, must be precise and all-embracing. Dressing rooms are allocated and the job of dressing and making-up the artistes is tackled in earnest. One dresser looks after the four artistes in dressing rooms 1 and 1A. Another dresser and an assistant attend to dressing room 3, which might have as many as eight artistes, and to dressing room 5, where Sam Pearson reigns alone. Make-up have doubled up their staff. Now four girls attend to the artistes as they arrive in groups to be made-up.

In the sophistication of the control room (compared with the spartan environment of the scanner) the director sits high above the studio floor, his back to the action, seeing only what the monitors carrying the cameramen's shots allow him to.

Alongside him in the control room sit the PA and the vision mixer, whose duties we shall look at in detail later. There is usually, too, a highly skilled technician whose function it is to ensure the smooth-running of the programme in all things technical. His title varies from company to company – operations manager, studio supervisor and so on – but we can refer to him here as the technical supervisor, since that describes in simple terms his responsibilities.

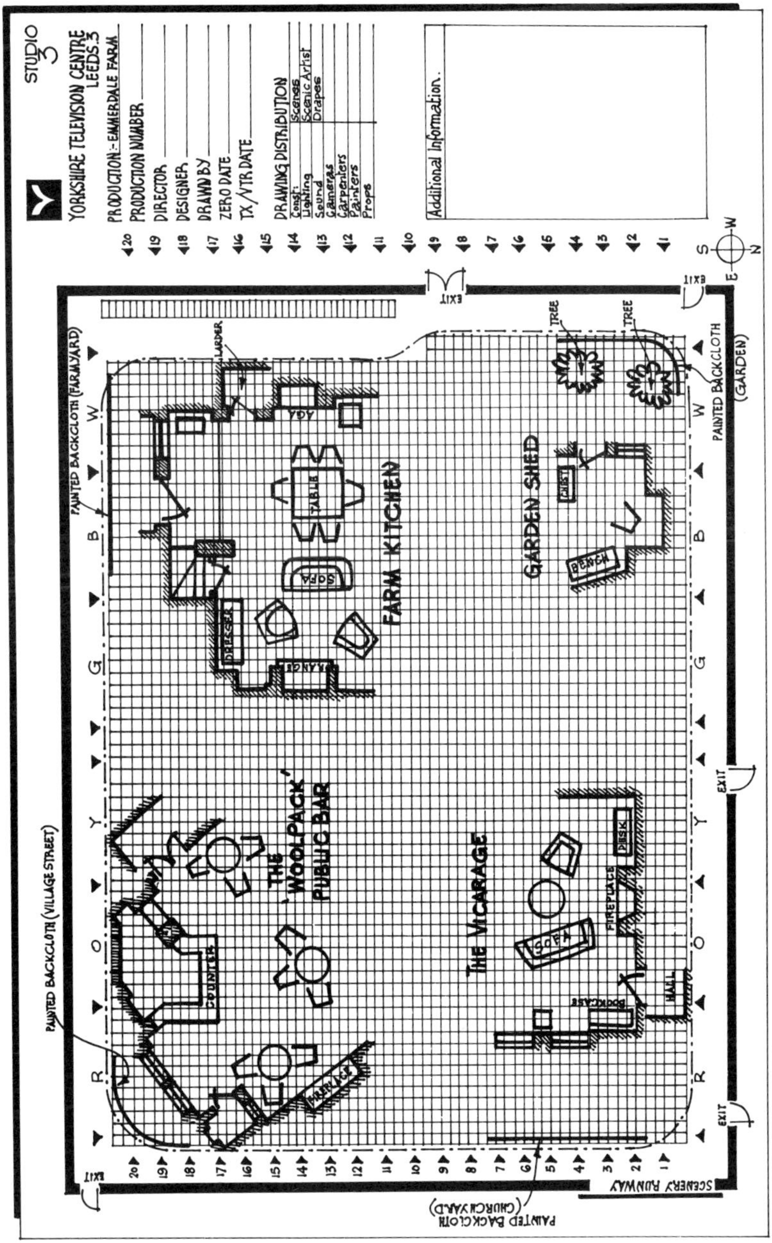

The studio floor plan for Emmerdale Farm.

The adjacent sound control room houses the sound supervisor, sitting at his vast bank of faders which enables him to control the level and quality of the sound from each of the microphones used on the programme. He is in constant touch with his team on the studio floor, particularly the 'boom operators' who shadow the artistes with their microphones, picking up every word they say. Alongside the supervisor there is usually an operator responsible for working the tape machines which provide the music and effects as and when they are needed.

In a further control room sit those responsible for picture quality. The lighting director is there of course, assisted by the console operator who activates the computerised bank of controls to provide the varying lighting effects required. In addition a very important technician – the vision control engineer – ensures that the cameras are 'tuned up' to provide the optimum in electronic quality, and also that the pictures from each camera match each other in quality, particularly in relation to colour. Without him a suit might look blue on one camera, purple on another and turquoise on a third. The designer usually sits in the vision control room for he works hand in glove with the lighting director, and the make-up girl is usually found there, checking the outcome of her efforts.

Rehearse, record. Rehearse, record. One by one the scenes are captured on video tape. The cameras are mounted on noiseless, easily moved 'dollies', and the cameramen, trained to work surely and

A sound supervisor at his control panel.

quickly, offer the shot required of them and then reposition for the next. Rehearse, record. The process continues.

As the artistes are called to the studio for their next scene, a wardrobe assistant checks their costumes one more time for continuity. Always continuity must be checked so that scenes shot out of sequence will look right when joined together.

EDITING

And joining together is the next step. When all the scenes have been shot they must be unravelled and placed in the correct order in the right episode. This is where the video tape editor earns his money. In his editing suite he loads an unused tape onto a machine. Other machines carry the tapes containing the early scenes of the first episode to be assembled. The best take of the first scene is recorded onto the virgin tape. Another tape carries the best take of the second scene and this, too, is transferred to the recording tape, butting onto the end of scene one. Naturally it is not as simple as that. Even with carefully prepared recordings much fine adjusting must be done electronically to join scene to scene, gradually building up the complete episode in such a way that it should look as if the whole programme has been shot as it happened in one glorious 'take'.

Edit follows edit. By the time all six episodes are ready for transmission the director and his PA and the video tape editors will spend something like ten hours a day over four days in the windowless confines of the edit suite, checking their notes, locating the tapes carrying the next scene needed, manipulating the edits over and over again until they are satisfied that no-one should 'spot the join'.

Months and months of planning, tens of thousands of typed words, acres of paper, immeasurable effort, technical expertise and talent have at last produced six episodes of *Emmerdale Farm*, each running about twenty-four minutes. While these very episodes were being edited over long hours in the edit suite, the next six were being shot in the studio and out on location. More dialogue to be learnt, more costumes ironed, more problems, challenges .. more hard work.

It might be difficult to believe, but this rough breakdown of how the soap opera is made to reach the screens each week has been ruthlessly pruned to avoid burying the reader in mounds of detail. People's involvement and responsibilities have only been touched on in many instances, but, hopefully, something has been conveyed of the complexity of the operation, and some measure of understanding reached as to how the pieces of the jigsaw are made to fit.

Emmerdale Farm, like all soap operas, becomes a juggernaut driving through a television company's facilities and schedules, brushing all aside as it heads for its destination. It drags along with it a whole industry, a whole lifestyle, almost, for those involved. It is – it has to be

– an extremely well-oiled, professional operation. From the planning which started a year before, to the episode being wound onto the video tape machine for transmission in less than an hour's time, hundreds of people have been involved. Despite strikes, snow and ice, breakdowns, sickness and all the other factors which could bring it to a halt it keeps going. Who can say if it will ever stop?

6 NO SECOND CHANCE

We have seen that the majority of television programmes these days are recorded, edited and transmitted on video tape. This enables the programme-maker to rehearse and record his programme scene by scene, item by item, recording again and again those scenes which are not to his satisfaction. Then the best version of each scene is joined to the best of the next scene in a pre-determined order to produce the finished play or musical spectacular the viewer eventually sees at home. On edited programmes, then, it is rightfully assumed that actors should never forget their lines, dancers make no mistakes, that pictures are properly composed and focused, and that when people speak they are heard.

Television was not always like that. Before anyone developed a reliable system for recording television programmes onto video tape, all television programmes, except those on film, were transmitted live as they happened. If an actor forgot his lines, or a dancer tripped and crashed through the scenery, the disaster was there on the screens at home for the viewer to see. Programmes did not have the polish and perfection which we have come to expect these days. For that unpredictable imp – human error – was always lurking, waiting to disrupt the most well-rehearsed of programmes. In addition, the complicated, intricate equipment needed to present television to the waiting millions was fallible, like everything else man-made. For the programme-makers, technicians and artistes, however, it was an exciting time. For no matter how much effort went into preparing and rehearsing a programme this could all be undone if mistakes occurred during transmission. There was no opportunity to re-shoot a scene; to replace a fallen wig and restart a love scene; no second chance at anything.

It is difficult to convey the sheer strain and nervous tension surrounding the rehearsals and transmission of a live play involving one-and-a-half hours of continuous action. For the artistes the demands on their acting ability were enormous. Not for them the luxury of learning and performing a play one small scene at a time. They had to know their lines, the performance expected of them, the position of every camera in relation to any scene they were involved in, and the nature of the shot each camera took at any time for the whole of the play – perfectly.

The same standards of perfection were demanded of the production team and technicians. A play of this nature might contain over seven

A studio scene from a play. In the days of 'live' plays the actors had no second chance.

hundred different shots, all carefully planned and rehearsed, each new shot numbered in sequence as follows.

Shot 8 on camera 3, close up Emily;
Shot 9 on camera 2, medium long shot of door as bell rings;
Shot 10 on camera 3, medium shot Emily, pan with her as she runs into kitchen;
Shot 11 on camera 1, medium shot from behind Edward as he enters and looks around empty room . . . and so on.

These shots, laid out in more abbreviated form than that of course, were marked on the script exactly where each would be needed to complement the dialogue and action of the artistes.

An actor who forgot to look to the right camera for an important close-up, or a cameraman who had dragged his camera to another set forgetting that he still had one more shot to take in the set he had just left, could throw the play into the sort of chaos from which it might never fully recover.

Cameramen became adept at composing new shots, quickly, accurately and artistically; at moving their cameras towards the action without losing focus, and of framing their shots instinctively. They followed the movement of artistes without losing them from the picture, and they devised means of marking cards attached to their cameras in such a way that they could instantly find the next shot needed from them during the play, what kind of shot it was, and where in relation to the action in should be taken from.

They marked the floor of the studio with chalk, so that they could place their cameras on the exact spot required for any shot with the minimum of delay. They learnt to move their equipment noiselessly around the studio at great speed, and with unerring accuracy. They were expected to do all these things during transmission with certainty, skill and sensitivity, and this they usually did, for they were well chosen and carefully trained.

The same applied to everyone else engaged on the production: sound technicians, vision mixers, stage hands and so on. Although these same skills are demanded of all those employed in making recorded television programmes today, the pressures are not as great as those experienced by those engaged on live programmes before the development of video tape. The sense of immediacy is missing. There is the knowledge that mistakes during recordings can be rectified.

The days of artistes changing their costumes as they ran from set to set are over. Present-day drama-makers find it hard to believe that in the 1950s when the BBC repeated the *Sunday Play* on the following Wednesday, the play was performed again and transmitted *live* with everyone involved hoping to repeat or improve on their performances of the previous Sunday. So those early days bred a race of television professionals who could make programmes, quite complicated programmes, under these difficult and tense conditions *and who got it right most of the time*. Those who could not stand the pace left the industry – fast.

Then along came the most important development in television for many, many years – video tape recording – and television has never been the same since. At last a programme-maker could record a scene, or a whole programme, and view the results immediately. If not to his liking he could (time permitting) record it all over again and again until satisfied. In addition, the quality of the recording was so high that the average viewer could not distinguish it from a live programme. Later, sophisticated techniques and equipment were developed which enabled the programme-maker to edit his scenes together in such a way that not even his professional colleagues could tell where these joins had been made.

Probably the most important change that the introduction of video tape brought to the television industry was that programmes no longer had to be made at the time they were transmitted. A dozen simple programmes lasting ten minutes each, say, and scheduled to be transmitted at 11 pm each evening for twelve nights, could be recorded in one long day in a studio. These would then be transmitted by a technician operating a video tape machine while those who made the programme were tucked up in bed.

A typical scene of activity during studio shooting.

During the following few days that same studio where the late night programmes had been made could then be used for recording all the interior scenes for a batch of six episodes of *Emmerdale Farm*, for example.

So programmes could be recorded when studio space, artistes, technical crews and production teams were available, irrespective of the time and date on which the programme would be transmitted. To the 'old timers' of television, however, those who had survived and thrived on those days and nights of live programmes, the coming of video tape took away much of the thrill and the exciting uncertainty of television. There are many, many people engaged in television today who have never experienced that mixture of excitement, terror, and the intoxication of adrenalin during those few moments before 'going on the air' with a major live programme.

Not all television programmes are recorded, however. There are still quite a few which are transmitted live, usually because of their topical nature. We shall be looking in greater detail at two excellent examples – *World of Sport* and *Grandstand* – in a later chapter. All news bulletins, early evening news magazine programmes, and many sporting outside broadcasts are still transmitted as they happen, mistakes and all.

There is an atmosphere surrounding the rehearsal and transmission of these types of programmes that is missing from recorded shows. This atmosphere is generated by the knowledge that, whatever the state of readiness of those engaged on the programme, there is a time set for the commencement of transmission that cannot be delayed.

At one minute and twenty-five seconds past 6 pm that programme will be transmitted to the waiting millions, come what may. Nothing jerks people out of their lethargy more than a PA saying 'thirty seconds to On Air'. No time to rehearse that tricky little section; forget about that caption that has only just arrived for the opening sequence; get make-up out of shot – the presenter will have to settle for his hair the way it is. Nothing, but nothing, stops the pulsating second-hand of the studio clock as it beats its way to the 'on air' time. We shall look in great detail at this type of programme later. For everyone engaged on productions like these the immediacy of television is very potent. There is also the knowledge that if something goes wrong it stays wrong until rescued.

Television veterans revel in stories of past disasters on live programmes; hilarious in retrospect, terrifying at the time. There are hundreds of them. Like chairs collapsing when artistes sat on them; scenery crashing over in the middle of a tender farewell to shouts of 'Look out!' and 'Behind you!'; the props man who was too late to run out of the set after moving a prop and who spent the rest of the scene under the dining room table where he had hurriedly taken refuge; the elephant, who, in front of millions of viewers . . . and so it goes on.

There was, in fact, all the fun and fear of the live theatre on the studio floor, with the added complications of television coverage and the wayward behaviour of electronic gadgetry. There have also been some tragic examples of the ruthlessness of live television. During transmission of a live drama from a London studio one of the actors died. His fellow actors, the studio personnel, and those in the control rooms had little option but to carry on with the play, improvising as they went along. That instance is by no means the only one on record, but, thankfully, such cases are extremely rare.

Nowadays, of course, programmes are assembled more often than not in the suites of video tape editors, whose sophisticated equipment can often help them rescue less than successful recordings and enhance the appeal of performances which just fell a little short of excellent on the day. Perhaps there is nothing wrong with that. What matters is the quality of the end-product so far as the viewer is concerned, and what use is technology in a technological industry if it cannot be used to advantage?

Nevertheless there is little to compare with coming off air knowing that it was good; knowing that it was right first time; knowing that it had to be right first time, for there was no second chance.

7 GATHERING THE NEWS

When looking at the area of live programming it is natural for the viewer to think only of news bulletins, and who can blame him. The idea of recorded news programmes is as unthinkable as catching up on the news by reading yesterday's newspapers. The bulletins may, and do, contain pre-recorded material, but it is essential that this material is presented to the viewer by a newscaster who is broadcasting live. How else can the information he imparts be as up-to-date as possible, even if the pictures illustrating a story are a few hours old?

It is not only news bulletins which are transmitted live. Daily news magazines, which offer more than just news, are transmitted live by ITV companies. Many current affairs events, too, are covered as they happen, as is much sport and major state occasions like the Royal Wedding. There is no doubt, however, that the majority of programmes which are *consistently* transmitted live originate from the department which produces daily news bulletins, news magazines and current affairs programmes.

There is never a slack day for those employed in this area of television. Since news happens constantly it is their function to gather this news and present it to the viewer as quickly as possible and in the most interesting and visual form. Television companies, then, have a well organised network of reporters and camera crews equipped to reach a location fast, film or video tape the item in the most interesting manner, and get this material back to the studios as quickly as possible. There, people are waiting to take this raw coverage of an event, edit the shots in the right order to tell the story in the most concise but dramatic manner, and write whatever introductions and commentaries the items might need.

Formerly, news items were always shot on film which had then to be processed before it could be handed over to the film editor to be cut according to instructions. This took time, a commodity in short supply in a television newsroom, and film was always liable to be scratched or even ruined by a fault in the processing machine.

Then along came ENG (electronic news gathering) which opened new doors for television newsmen. ENG does not involve the use of film. Instead the two-man news unit carry a compact video camera with its own recording unit. Pictures and sound are recorded direct onto a video cassette which can be viewed immediately on the unit's monitor. This cassette can then either be despatched to the newsroom for instant editing, or, if the crew are a great distance from the studios, the cassette can be taken to a pre-arranged nearby location and transmitted back to the newsroom where it is recorded and immediately thereafter edited.

ENG has the added dimension of enabling coverage of an event to be 'fed' into a live programme, once a television link has been established between the ENG unit and the television studio. An exciting news story is given added potency when the newsreader can say, 'And now, for the latest information on the state of the people trapped on the roof of that blazing hotel, let's go live to our man on the spot, John Smith.' Also using ENG equipment, teams can travel to other countries, record an event, and by the use of land lines and satellites beam the pictures back to their home country. Little wonder, then, that television news gatherers viewed ENG as probably the most significant technical advance in the past decade.

ITN in London has the responsibility of providing a national news service to the whole of the ITV network. The BBC also has a responsibility to provide national news programmes, and they can call on the experience gained over many years of broadcasting in both radio and television. Both ITN and the BBC have developed a reliable system of getting hold of any newsworthy pictures from anywhere in the world and passing these back to London where they can take their place in the next available programme. Both these organisations provide regular news bulletins througbout the day, including weekends, with the

An ENG crew in action covering a demonstration.

late evening news being their main showcase. ITN also supplies items of local interest to other ITV companies and receives items of national importance from them. The BBC has a similar set-up with its regional studios.

These two providers of national news programmes are now extremely professional in their approach to their responsibilities, and they have both developed a highly sophisticated expertise in their specialised field. They are geared to provide news flashes at very short notice. They mount marathon productions at such times as general elections, using the latest technology, visual displays, outside locations, informed opinion, up-to-the-minute results, analyses, and interviews with politicians and others who have been pitch-forked into the limelight.

The regions are also served on a local basis by both ITV and the BBC. The newsrooms of these localised organisations are authorities on the news potential of their particular areas. Little that happens within their locality escapes them. They know who the personalities of the region are, the stories behind industry and commerce, the geography, and road, rail and air systems, the stories behind the stories.

In a visual medium like television, the newsroom staff are constantly striving to *show* the viewer the news rather than simply report it. For that reason they employ a number of news camera teams, depending on the size of the company and the area it covers. These are usually compact units consisting of camerman, sound recordist and reporter, although this varies from company to company.

These units are despatched, often at short notice, to where the news is happening. Their function is to capture the incident as quickly, competently and dramatically as possible, and get the story back to the studios with the minimum of delay. Major companies place staff news-units strategically throughout their region to enable them to cover the news, wherever it breaks. As a back-up, most companies also have a pool of freelance cameramen and reporters, called 'stringers', who can be called on when there is more work than the staff crews can handle. Stringers are only paid, therefore, when they shoot material which is used on a programme, and for that reason they are constantly on the look-out for good stories and news items which will interest the newsroom and therefore get them assignments.

These stringers live in the areas they represent. Everyone knows them locally, and they are an invaluable source of information when it comes to items of local news. They get to hear things strangers would not hear; they drink at the local pubs; taxi drivers pass on items of gossip to them; they are in the know when it comes to highly localised affairs, and no television newsroom could function without them.

Sometimes they stumble on items of national, even international significance. Some years ago a television journalist working for a regional company was making his early morning calls to the stringers in his area, checking on any news items they might have for him. Knowing that one particular cameraman was quite ill with 'flu' he nearly did not ring – but habit prevailed, and in any event he wanted to know when the man might be fit enough to resume work. The stringer's wife answered the telephone. She said that her husband had received a call a few minutes earlier which had caused him to leave his sick bed and race out of the house with his camera, despite the fact that he was running a temperature of over 100° F.

The journalist, quite obviously, realised that something big had happened. He rang the local police and was told to get off the line. It was the same with the emergency services. He rang the cameraman's wife again and asked her if she knew where her husband had gone. She mentioned a little-known village in the mining valleys of South Wales, and a reporter from the studio was immediately despatched to the scene. The village was Aberfan, and within minutes the horrific story began to emerge that a waterlogged coal tip had collapsed, engulfing a school and killing over a hundred young children. It was a story which stunned and shocked the world, and touched the hearts of parents everywhere. But it was to the local stringer that the initial telephone call was made by an eye-witness, not to the regional television company, less than 30 miles down the road.

Happily, such tragic instances are comparatively rare, and news coverage for both staff units and stringers is a fairly routine business. Politicians have to be interviewed; a new hospital wing opened; a barn fire filmed. They have unpleasant tasks, too, like filming the aftermath of multiple road crashes, murder investigations, harrowing funerals and unbearable grief. Although they do develop an apparent hardness to cocoon them from some of the awfulness of life, it is not unknown for crews to break down in distressing situations, particularly when they can do nothing to help someone in their moment of agony or pain.

It is a hard school, professionally, too, for they rarely have the chance to shoot a news item twice; they must get it right first time. For that reason it is good training for the future. The cameraman, for instance, soon develops an instinct for the essential ingredients of an incident or story, and learns to shoot fast, accurately and dramatically, often in uncomfortable surroundings. Some of them go on to become top documentary cameramen as a result of this grounding.

The roving teams of camera crews and reporters of ITN and BBC in London are prepared to go anywhere in the world and at any time to where the stories are – to where the hot news is happening. They are backed up by their company's correspondents in most of the major countries in the world, who have acquired the necessary contacts and local knowledge of their environment which enables them to present informed reports on stories emanating from their particular country. In fact, so well oiled is the television coverage of events from all over the world that the viewer has become accustomed to seeing them on his screens in the next scheduled news bulletin, and feels rather let down if they are not there.

Over the years television news gatherers have brought some dramatic and moving events into our living rooms. The tragic, fatal end to Donald Campbell's attempt on the world water speed record; the massacre by El Salvador troops of demonstrators clustered on the steps of a cathedral; the horrors of wars that are constantly raging somewhere in the world; Royal visits; sporting achievements – we now take them all for granted. Millions watched in anguish as an air hostess, one of the survivors of the Washington air crash in 1981, appeared to lose the will to live and seemed certain to vanish beneath the icy waters of the Potomac river. Then came the heart-stopping seconds when a passer-by plunged into the numbingly cold water and dragged her to safety. No amount of words, however well written, could hope to match those pictures of drama and heroism brought into our living rooms by the cameras of American television news crews. It is with visual presentation in mind that television news units travel thousands of miles each year to bring us the stories which reflect life on this planet.

Life, of course, is not all disaster. Cameras covering the globe-trotting Pope John Paul brought us emotional, sometimes intensely beautiful, scenes as he was greeted by the faithful; bravery and endeavour were encapsulated in the shots of *Gipsy Moth*, with Francis Chichester at the helm, rounding Cape Horn in towering seas; and the poignant scenes as the American hostages from Iran were reunited with their loved ones brought a lump to many a throat.

Sometimes, however, the men who bring us the news become news themselves, like the three-man ITN crew who turned up after three months without trace in a hostile African state, having been given up for dead by many people.

Living close to death is often a daily experience for these teams. Being a television cameraman or reporter does not grant anyone immunity from the bomb or the bullet; quite often the reverse is the case. The very privilege granted to camera crews to go where the public are forbidden often places them in the kind of danger the average viewer will never experience in his life. Standing alongside soldiers in Belfast who are being bombarded with bricks and petrol bombs is a terrifying and dangerous experience. To continue to cover the action in the midst of this mayhem demands professionalism and courage of the highest order from the cameraman, sound recordist and the reporter.

It is all too common for suspicious and ruthless representatives of alien countries to beat up news crews, throw them into filthy cells, even to kill them. An American crew filming their reporter talking to troops in a South American state were horrified to see their colleague casually, and for no apparent motive, shot dead in front of their lens. A

British film crew in Argentina during the Falklands crisis were convinced they were to be executed by the police when they were bundled into a car at gunpoint and driven out into the country beyond Buenos Aires. In the end they were roughed-up, stripped and abandoned – but it might have been worse. During the occupation of what is now Kampuchea the Kmer Rouge soldiers had no qualms about killing newsmen.

We tend to forget, too, that film crews run the same risk of mutilation and death as the soldiers they are filming during times of war . . . without the benefit of a gun to protect them. Furthermore, there are many wars being fought all the time somewhere in the world. One ITN reporter decided to quit his roving assignments after covering thirteen wars in what the average British viewer would regard as a period of peace. Reporters are occasionally provided with bullet-proof vests, so great are the dangers they sometimes have to face.

The courage of these crews is often remarkable. There are a number of cases where cameramen have continued to film right up to the second they were killed. Such an instance happened on an airstrip in Guyana some years ago when a Fact-Finding Mission investigating the religious settlement set up by the fanatical Jimmy Jones came under fire. The cameraman continued to film as the guns were turned on him, fatally wounding him, as millions of viewers witnessed when his film was eventually shown.

These news crews often suffer much privation; there are few comforts if you are filming with the Afghanistan rebels in the mountains, or wading ashore with landing troops in the Falklands. Hilton hotels, too, are thin on the ground in the African jungle, or the wastes of Alaska.

Why they do it is something they might find difficult to explain themselves. The cynical reply is to say that it is for the money, but thoughts of money are far from a cameraman's mind when he is looking down the wrong end of an Armelite rifle in the hands of a fanatic. The motivation is complex, but it can probably best be summed up by saying that it is the thrill of it all. The thrill of being where the big news is happening; to be in the forefront of the action; to get pictures that are exciting, or moving, or startling, or out of the ordinary. There is an egotistical motive, too, if the crews are honest with themselves, for there is an intense professional satisfaction in coming back with the item whatever the hardships or dangers, perhaps where lesser men might have failed – and who wants a nine-to-five job anyway?

Keeping abreast of what is happening regionally, nationally and internationally is the responsibility of the news editor. No item of news which might interest his viewers should ever escape his eagle eye, and it rarely does. If he works for a company providing television to the West of England, say, he must have a network of information which will make him aware of anything interesting which will happen in that area. He knows, of course, that his viewers are also interested in national and international events, and although these will be covered by the major networked news bulletins he must not ignore them if they have any local significance to the viewers in the West of England.

The news editor is usually on the scene early each day so that he can quickly acquaint himself with what is happening in his area. He must decide which items of news are worth following up, which reporter shall be assigned to the job, how each item should be treated, what form it is likely to take in the finished programme, how long the item will probably run, and what its priority is in relation to other news events of that day.

Newsrooms keep a diary listing known events which are to happen in the days and weeks ahead. Such things as visits by Royalty to that television company's area, the launching of a ship, a pop festival, the ceremonial opening of a large store by a famous film star, an important conference taking place in the region, the proposed publishing of a major report affecting the future of industry in the area, the blowing up of a tall chimney (always a great favourite with viewers and cameramen), or an important sporting event – all are listed for future attention.

In addition, a journalist is usually delegated to list those news stories which have only come to light that morning, or which 'broke' overnight. Newspapers, too, are carefully scanned for any item which should receive the television newsman's attention. Stringers throughout the area telephone in with items of interest. In one corner, telex machines carrying news reports from the Press Association chatter constantly, printing these news items often within minutes of their occurrence. In television newsrooms all over the country the same reports are received, evaluated and either followed up or discarded depending on the interest these items might or might not have for the viewers in that television area.

Soon, at 10 am say, the producer of the day, or of the next news programme, calls a meeting to assess the stories, features and news items available to him, and to decide on the composition of the programme he will eventually produce. For the time being, however, the main function of the newsroom is finding out what is happening and where, and getting people out to the scene – fast.

In the case of the BBC and ITN in London, they will be studying the international scene with great interest. If there is a major news story somewhere which they cannot get their own crews to cover in time, like the dramatic rescue in the Potomac river of the air hostess, then they call upon the specialists within their organisation to arrange for the American pictures to be beamed by satellite to England. Because the American system of producing television pictures is different from ours, and therefore cannot be viewed on our screens, these have to be converted to the television system we use before they can be edited and eventually transmitted.

The time differences throughout the world between countries must be taken into account, of course, when booking facilities from other companies abroad.

Where a major story breaks in another country which will need following-up in the days to come, then the company's correspondent in that country is usually flown to the scene to provide the specialised reporting required by his organisation. There, usually with his own crews and in constant touch with the newsroom back in England, he is available to give his news editor the coverage he wants, the interview he requests, the explanatory commentary and the in-vision piece to camera which not only usefully sums up the situation with the appropriate foreign scene in the background, but which also gives the company the prestige value of showing that they have their man on the spot giving the latest reports and updating the news. They all derive a certain pride from including the now-familiar 'This is Jon Snow, for News at Ten, with the Guerrillas in El Salvador . . .', or 'Christopher Morris, from the White House, Washington'.

It is a well-known adage that nothing is as stale as yesterday's news, and life goes on whatever the tragedies and triumphs. What was so important yesterday, so worthwhile breaking the speed limit to reach or risking one's life for has been shot, edited and transmitted. Today another story has hit the headlines. It is time to stow the gear aboard the truck and get to where it is happening. Such is the life of the newscameraman, and sometimes, just sometimes, something happens which puts it all into perspective.

One cameraman, with the experience of fourteen wars behind him, found himself in Belfast on an assignment for one of the major television organisations. An officer attempting to defuse a bomb had been blown up, and it was clear that a new method of countering any attempt to defuse the device was in use. Now, a similar bomb had been located, and an officer was prepared to tackle the highly dangerous task of attempting to render it harmless, knowing that a fellow officer had died in a similar attempt.

The cameraman was asked to cover this attempt. In view of the location of the bomb the only logical way to do this was to get right up to the device with the expert – which he did. For two days they were together while the officer worked to defuse the bomb. As he worked, the cameraman filmed, their lives hung in the balance, and the shots the cameraman took were highly dramatic.

Eventually the officer defused the device and the cameraman despatched the film to London. Later, he received a telephone call from the company. It seemed that all but a few feet of the film had been rendered unusable by a fault on the processing plant. The company was, naturally, very apologetic and thanked him for his efforts. The cameraman (a family man with five children) immediately packed his bags, left Belfast, and never covered another war or placed himself in mindless danger again.

Having acquired the news material, be it film or ENG tape, there is the very important matter of how best to use it. The decision depends on a number of factors, such as the news editor's opinion of the news value of the story, and that often depends on the value of other news items which have broken that day. A story which would be treated as the main item one day – say a hunt for a missing girl – would be relegated in importance if a plane crashed onto a housing estate during the afternoon.

Events are rarely as dramatic as that, however. Often the treatment a story will receive is decided before the reporting team leave the building. Some items are worth only about twenty or thirty seconds of film with a commentary – 'mute film with voice over', as it is called. Other stories deserve more attention. In those cases the film will run longer in its edited form, with sound effects recorded on the location, and it will probably include an interview or two with the people most involved in the story.

Sometimes on magazine programmes the item has such interest that it becomes more than a news story and is elevated in importance to a major item. In this case the story commences with an introduction by a studio presenter, followed by the film, eventually a discussion in the studio when the 'fors and againsts' can air their views. The item may be further 'dressed' by the addition of slides and captions, or by the inclusion of library film if relevant to the treatment.

Occasionally a story assumes a loftier rating than originally envisaged because the material shot by the news crew is so good that it is worth devoting more time to the item. Sometimes the reverse is the case! In any event the film or tape reaches the editor as soon as possible and a member of the news team (the actual reporter who went out on the assignment if possible) is delegated to view the material, assess its worth, and then supervise the editing of the film or tape to the length of time allocated by the news editor or the producer of the programme.

If there are facilities and time, extra sound effects and further commentary are added. More often than not, for there is never enough time to do everything on a news programme, the extra commentary is read by a reporter in the studio as the item is being transmitted.

It is a fairly common occurrence for late items to be edited for inclusion in a programme even after that programme has gone On Air. Once the item has been cut there follows a frantic dash along corridors by one of the younger members of the team to get the material to the film or ENG machines as soon as possible, ready for inclusion in the programme. At the same time a reporter informs the studio control-room team of the running-time of the edited item and of any points they must look out for when they transmit the story: how long studio commentary should last before fading up the sound recorded on the film or tape; or where it is necessary to superimpose a caption giving the name and status of a person being interviewed, such as 'Superintendent Plodd, Head of Regional Crime Squad'.

Instances like the above illustrate another advantage of ENG over film. Films for a programme are joined together in the order in which they are scheduled to be shown, and the resulting large reels loaded onto telecine machines before the programme goes on the air. Once loaded, it is impossible to 'drop in' another film story without removing the reel, taking it back to the editor, spinning the reel until the position for the new story is found, splicing that item into the reel, taking the reel back to the operator who then reloads it into his machine. By this time the programme would be off the air and the other films on the reel doomed never to be seen.

ENG has changed that. Once ENG has been edited it emerges as a self-contained cassette. This can be taken to the ENG technician who loads it into his machine in seconds wherever it is required by the producer. This flexibility with late items is what television lacked in the days when film was the only means of giving news items any visual treatment. Now, television is virtually as flexible as radio when it comes to late items, much to the delight of newsroom staff whose journalistic background caused them to rebel when a good late story could not be included in its full glory because of the restrictions of television film requirements.

Some viewers wonder why it is almost standard practice to use two newscasters to read a news bulletin; not always, but usually. One very good reason is that news bulletins contain stories which embrace the whole range of human experience – death, humour, despair, triumph, tragedy, success and failure. It is extremely difficult for one newscaster to change the mood of his delivery when reading successive stories of contrasting impact. Imagine the change of style required between delivering a story on the happy reaction of a man who has just won a world-record amount on the pools and a harrowing account of the plight of the starving millions in Ethiopia. It is unnatural for the reader to wipe the smile off his face at the end of the first story and assume a grave posture for the second. It is neater and more acceptable to leave the smiling newscaster and cut to another whose serious demeanour prepares the viewer for the change of mood.

In some television companies the news stories are written for the newsreaders by journalists working on the news desk. Other organisations expect the newscasters themselves to provide the words. Both systems seem to work quite well, although the former method is probably better in companies whose reporters are out on location most of the day, gathering film or tape items, and who arrive back at the studios ready to appear live on the programme with little time to spare.

The free interchange of visual news material between television companies is a vital part of the set-up of any newsroom team. Granada TV might have an ENG item which is needed by Anglia TV for their evening news magazine programme. If Granada can co-operate in getting the item to Anglia it will, for it, too, might need a similar favour in the future, and there is a bond, anyway, between those who spend their lives in the newsrooms of the world. Usually there is no time for Granada to put the tape on a train to Norwich, and in any case it might not want to part with it just yet (needing it for its own local magazine programme). The logical alternative is to send the pictures along one of the land lines (an already established network of ground cables) which have been allocated for the use of television companies.

To achieve this transfer of material Granada must ensure that it has an ENG machine available to 'play out' the item. Anglia must endeavour to book a land line for a period long enough for the item to be sent and recorded, at the same time ensuring that it has a video machine in Norwich available to record the incoming item. It might sound a little pedestrian but it does work, and news items and other stories criss-cross the UK daily.

ITN reporters, too, when despatched to the regions to follow up a story of national importance, rely heavily on the goodwill of the television company holding the franchise for that area. If the reporter is covering a late morning story in Glasgow, for example, he can hardly expect to take it down to London, edit it and add commentary ready for transmission at 1 pm or 5.45 pm the same day. Instead he takes the material to Scottish Television who provide him with a desk and typewriter to enable him to write his commentary, and an editor who will cut the item for him. He has free use of the telephone so that he can keep his London office in the picture, and when the item is complete Scottish Television assists him in playing it down to London along the land lines as explained earlier.

In the same spirit of co-operation, ITN will do its best to get to Scottish Television, or any other company, such material as they might require. Sometimes (and this is every regional reporter's dream), ITN cannot get a man of their own to cover a local story and they then take the item the local reporter has made for his own company. Apart from getting their reports (and their faces) on the national news programme, regional reporters are aware that their performances are also being observed by the top men at ITN; and this can often lead to the advancement of their careers if they have any real talent. By some strange coincidence some of the top national and international reporters – Norman Rees, Martyn Lewis, Ken Rees and John Humphrys – all went to ITN and the BBC from the same regional company, TWW, later HTV, so fairy tales do happen.

Before being entrusted with overseas assignments, these ITN and BBC reporters each spent many years for their companies covering the length and breadth of the UK, often never knowing where they were to end up the next day until the evening before. It is immensely rewarding for the dyed-in-the-wool reporter, but it is a tough, demanding existence. It entails much travelling, and living out of suitcases, and puts a strain on family life.

Later they find themselves despatched abroad on short assignments, and eventually established, for a while at least, as the organisation's representative in America, or Africa, handling all the major stories which happen in those countries.

Finding, assembling and broadcasting the news deserves whole books dedicated to the subject. Many reporters, of course, have written their accounts of the life of a news gatherer, and fascinating reading much of it is. It is a life-style only for those who thrive on it. It is no place for anyone who simply treats it as a job and who is irritated when it interrupts his plans to go fishing, taking the kids to school, or going on holiday.

It often means going where they do not want to go, reporting stories they find harrowing and dangerous, and sometimes being shot at by people they have not even met, let alone offended. They must develop the ability to combine insight with speed when covering a story, and only those with a solid journalistic background, vast experience and such qualities as dedication, talent and determination need apply.

8 GETTING IT ON AIR

Major news programmes, like the BBC's *Nine O'clock News* and ITN's *News at Ten*, follow a well-defined format of one or two newscasters reading items of news, usually in the order of their importance in the opinion of the programme editor. These items are as well illustrated as the news team can make them. In addition to film and ENG contributions, there are video recordings of material supplied by other companies or regions, and, as we saw earlier, pictures and reports from other countries.

It is a static format with the newscaster sitting behind a desk, sometimes with a variety of backgrounds illustrating each particular story he reads. Occasionally he interviews a person in another part of the country via a monitor, or a recording of an earlier interview with someone in the news is shown. We are all familiar with this set-up, which is probably all that a news-only programme requires in the way of presentation.

Regional news magazine programmes, which have a blend of news, features, interviews, demonstrations, and even musical items, are just what their title suggests: visual magazines with a topical basis and a strong emphasis on items and features reflecting the life of the particular region concerned. These programmes require more preparation than the straightforward news bulletin, since they mirror a broader spectrum of life. In ITV, no two companies prepare and present their daily news magazines in exactly the same way, but there is a structure which roughly illustrates a typical day on such programmes, which, with one or two exceptions, are usually transmitted at 6 pm each weekday immediately following the early national news from ITN. BBC regions have their versions, and they also contribute to the networked news magazines.

For the men and women who work on these programmes much of the appeal lies in the fact that at the beginning of the day there is no programme – a blank piece of paper, if you like. Yet by 6 pm they must go on the air with a half-hour programme packed with interest and news for the viewers in their area. Then at 6.30 pm they can make their way home, hopefully professionally satisfied, knowing that tomorrow another blank sheet of paper waits to be filled; to be filled with stories that even then are starting to happen or which are yet to occur.

The staff who are responsible for gathering and editing the material, writing the scripts and presenting these programmes are usually drawn from a journalistic background. They are trained to assess the value of news stories, to hone these down to size, to write quickly and under pressure, and above all to meet deadlines whatever the problems and distractions along the way. As we shall see, having done this they hand over the scripts to the people who will convert their words into a practical television programme, the programme director and the studio crew. There is a great similarity between newspapers and this area of television, so it is logical for the programe to have an editor. He is the man responsible for the overall shape of the programme, its main policies, how it should reflect local life, what it will or will not do when controversial matters emerge; in short, the style.

Some editors occasionally produce these programmes; some never do. In any event, each day a producer is given the responsibility of filling that blank piece of paper which will eventually become a transmitted programme. A good editor does not interfere with the producer of the day. If a man has been given that responsibility he should be allowed to get on with it in his own way, and sink or swim professionally in the process. The editor is available, however, for consultation and advice, and he still has the overall authority to override a producer's decision if he feels it necessary.

The day starts, as we saw earlier, with the news staff checking on the main news items of that day, with film or ENG crews despatched to cover those that are urgent. At the same time, someone prepares a list of these stories, adding anything happening that day which might interest the producer as an item for the programme. Any story, be it local, national or international which might provide an item of interest to the viewers is included, and copies placed before everyone who attends the morning conference – the meeting, usually at about 10 am, where suggestions for filling that blank piece of paper will begin to shape the programme for that evening.

The programme editor attends, of course, together with the producer of the day. The all-important news editor and the team of journalists, reporters, presenters and researchers are there, together with the programme director who later that day will have the responsibility for the smooth running of the programme when it goes on air. In some companies, film and ENG editors are represented.

Usually the producer first asks the news editor for his resumé of news stories worth attention, for it is around these that the programme will be built. The news editor details these and lists those to which reporters and crews have been assigned or despatched. With the 'hard' news out of the way, the producer turns to those softer stories which might make longer features reflecting more on the manner of life within the region than with the short, sharp items of news which have broken that day. The morning conference is the place for anyone to suggest ideas for items, and in a busy, thriving news magazine set-up there is rarely any shortage of these.

A regional news room bustling with activity.

At this stage the producer begins to feel a pattern for the programme emerging as he considers the material available to him: make the main item the docks strike (say six minutes), to include some filmed reports from the docks followed by an interview with both sides in the studio; allow the news editor eight minutes, as it is a strong news day; a few minutes each for the battery pigs, the eighty-year-old road sweeper and the Tommy Steele interview; put in the rates row story if the councillor will come to the studio; and there is that football story, shot yesterday but right for showing today.

Of course, it is never that simple to plan and implement the ingredients of that evening's programme. Items which seemed so promising at 10 am collapse when further research reveals that the story is not as strong, interesting or as accurately portrayed as first appeared. Perhaps the one person vital to the shape or balance of the item cannot or will not agree to appear. It might be that a threatened strike does not materialise, or that a jury in an important court case does not produce a verdict when expected. It is not unknown, too, for rival companies to monopolise important interviewees.

Nevertheless the production team as they leave the morning conference at least are aware of what the producer's aspirations are, and what their individual responsibilities are to help him realise these. The office becomes alive with telephone calls, rattling typewriters, animated conversations. Rooms where these programmes are prepared are usually of the open-plan type so that the editor and producers can have ready access to the news desk, the reporters, researchers, directors and PAs, so there is much noise.

In one area, girls with headphones receive and type the stories coming in from reporters and stringers out in the field. Secretaries type incessantly: there are letters from viewers to be answered, internal memos, 'thank you' letters, confirmation of arrangements to be implemented, payments to guests, stringers and others to be authorised – the normal outgoings of a busy organisation. As the day progresses the pace quickens, and the level of noise increases. As some items fall by the wayside so others emerge as the never-ending supply of news stories continues. Film and video tape starts to arrive for editing, and from the editing rooms the sounds from half-a-dozen different stories compete with each other as the items are knocked into shape.

Yet this seemingly unrelated activity throughout the department is following a definite pattern dictated by the producer. By early afternoon he can be fairly certain in his own mind how he intends the programme to look. He knows what is available to him in the way of items and visuals; he knows who can or cannot appear; he has made up his mind what the shape of the programme will be, and that might well be quite different from his plans at 10.30 that morning.

It is time to put these thoughts onto paper, and the producer prepares a 'running order' which sets out the exact form he wants the programme to take. It will look like the following, with presenters Tom, Dick, Harry and Harriet available to him that day.

Opening slide with titles over studio shot.
Opening link, Tom, including slides and ENG.
DOCKS ITEM. Link Dick plus film and ENG into discussion, Dick + 2 guests.
NEWS. HARRY AND HARRIET including film, ENG, slides and captions.
ROAD SWEEPER. Tom link into ENG.
Link, Dick into commercial break. . . .

The rest of the programme will be laid out in a similar fashion.

This running order is then typed out neatly by the PA, and each item chronologically numbered. Copies are made and distributed throughout the office so that everyone engaged on the production is now in no doubt as to where and in what form his or her contribution will jigsaw its way into the overall structure of the programme. At the same time the news editor prepares *his* running order, maintaining control and balance over the avalanche and words and pictures pouring into his domain.

As each news items is typed in a rough fashion and then retyped into a more professional form by skilled typists, and as reporters and presenters write and rewrite their links and commentaries, there is a build-up of paper everywhere – reams and reams of it. Each finally-typed page is duplicated dozens of times and stacked on a long table alongside other piles of pages, with item four, for example, carefully placed between items three and five. When every item has been stacked in this way, girls walk along this line taking one page from each pile in numbered order, eventually arriving with a completed script which is then stapled and stacked ready for distribution. Dozens of copies are built up in this way for many people will need them if the programme is to be transmitted smoothly as planned.

Meanwhile, even before the scripts are collated, the director's role begins to emerge. He has a copy of the running order, and it is his function to make possible the programme which the producer wants. He must convert the ideas and expectations contained in the running order into practical television, for it is he, the director, who will channel the efforts of the technicians and operators to achieve this.

He must make the running order work, then, and it is worth looking at what this means. He has a limited number of cameras and microphones. The studio itself has four immovable walls, and the set can occupy only a certain part of it. Bearing these factors in mind, he goes through the running order like a game of chess, deciding where presenters will sit at any time to deliver their links or conduct their interviews, at the same time allocating those cameras and microphones needed to cover the action. One area of the studio might have to be used to accommodate more than one interview. A presenter having delivered his link into an item might then have to give up his desk to a colleague to read the news a little later in the programme. Towards the end of an interview one camera will have to be pulled away and moved to another part of the studio ready to cover the next item immediately the interview ends.

All these requirements go through the director's mind as he juggles with the resources at his disposal. He knows which camera can best cover any given part of the set without intruding into other camera's shots or becoming entangled in their cables. He has become skilled at knowing how to deploy all the available technical facilities and skills to provide a polished programme along the lines laid down by the producer, and to enhance it if he can.

Having done all this he then meets up with the studio crews who will lay out the studio along the lines he has planned. Chairs, tables and props are shuffled about until the director is satisfied. The lighting director sets about the task of lighting each shot the director wishes to take on the programme. At the same time, the sound technicians set out the microphones for every position from which sound is required to be heard, plugging these into special wall sockets so that the sound from each of these microphones will find its way onto the sound supervisor's control desk. Here, a separate sliding 'fader' for each microphone gives the sound-chief control over every sound source needed on the programme. By sliding the fader up or down he can control the volume; by moving other knobs and switches he can influence the quality of the sound.

With the studio set for action, the director calls the whole crew together and goes through the running order in detail, making sure that every operator knows what his or her function will be when the programme is transmitted. For each item, then, the cameramen will note their particular involvement (camera one on close-ups of interviewer, camera two on a wide shot, camera three on close-ups of interviewees, for example). Similarly the sound men will note which microphones are involved, the lighting director which lighting effects are required, and the vision mixer which special effects, mixes or electronic transmissions from camera to camera she must implement.

Then every shot the director is likely to take during the programme is looked at and checked for picture quality, with members of the studio crew sitting in for absent participants. Fast camera moves from one area to another are tested 'against the clock', lighting changes checked, intricate visual and aural sequences rehearsed until they are flawless. In short anything and everything which might happen on the programme is tried and tested. Nothing is left to chance in the hope that it might work on the night.

The running order sets out the pattern of the programme for that evening, but the script provides the detail from which the director and his team will work. Where the running order said simply 'link Tom into film' the script will contain the actual words Tom will say together

Five minutes to 'on air' for the presenter.

with details of the film with room for each member of the team to make their individual notes. We shall see later how this script is marked up and interpreted by different members of the studio team.

In the meantime the PA has been busy timing each presenter's link, report, or news story, ascertaining the length of each film and video insert, and checking with the producer just how much time he intends to allocate to each interview in the programme. Having gathered all this information she is in a position to tell him that his programme will run, say, thirty-five minutes and twenty seconds. If the programme has been scheduled to run for thirty-three minutes and ten seconds (no more, no less) then he must make cuts in the programme immediately – perhaps removing one or two news stories and shortening a link, or reducing the time he has allocated to an interview. Sometimes all this is completed only minutes, occasionally seconds, before the programme is due to go on air, for on live, highly topical programmes like these producers like to keep their options open as late as possible to accommodate last-minute items of news and hot-from-the-camera pictures.

In the darkened control room with its banks of monitors at last all is ready. There is one minute to go to 'on air'. The studio settles down with a tense calmness. The PA counts down the seconds to go ... 'forty-five seconds to on air' ... 'thirty seconds to on air' ... 'twenty seconds'.... The director looks around and checks that everyone is poised, 'stand by with the opening music' ... 'coming to slide first, then camera two with caption' (the vision mixer nods her confirmation), 'stand by for your lighting change' (he glances at the lighting director in his control room and gets a thumbs-up), 'opening link from Tom then into docks item' (Tom at his desk in the studio hears the director through his earpiece and nods).

The PA's voice overrides everyone's thoughts ... 'ten seconds to on air, nine, eight, seven, six, five ...'.

9 FOUR, THREE, TWO, ONE, ZERO.

'Cue music ... coming to two ... take two ... zoom out ... super caption ... go lighting change ... coming to Tom next on three ... start fading the music ... coming to three ... mix and cue Tom ...'. The programme is on the air. There is no stopping and going back if things are not quite right; no waiting until a camera gets to the next shot; no letting-up of concentration; no escaping the relentless second-hand of the clock as the thirty-three minutes and ten seconds of the programme running-time tick away.

At times like these the director is very much like the conductor of an orchestra: cueing this instrument now, lowering the volume of that, glancing towards another as a stand-by warning, controlling the pace, the mood, the style; encouraging, driving, chastising, but always authoritative.

In the example below, the asterisks show at exactly which point in the presenter's speech the director gives his instructions.

Director	*Presenter*
Stand by to take docks slide ...	Good evening. In a moment we'll be looking at the big story
Take slide* ... coming back to three	of the day ... the docks* strike, as the solution seems further
Take three* ... stand by slide of Tommy Steele	away than ever.* We'll also be meeting an eighty-year old man who refuses to retire, and
Take slide* ... coming back to three ... take three.* Coming to one ... take one.* Cue Dick.	chatting to one* of our most popular entertainers who seems to get younger every year.* But first ... here's Dick.*

So it goes on throughout the programme, with the director calling his instructions, preparing people for their next task, striving for perfection from everybody, trying to lift performances, to attain the optimum in effort and skill: 'coming to two, cut, zoom in ... slower ... slower ... good! hold it there ... nicely done Jim ... coming to slide and music ... take it ... hold the music down ... down! that's fine ... right let it go great! stand by, Harriet ... dip the music ... mix to two ... good ... coming to one next ... a little tighter ... fine ... kill music, take one ... cue Harriet ... cameras three and two clear to interview ... well done, everyone ... stand by, Tom.'

The director has marked his script along the following lines. The underlining and oblique strokes show exactly which point in the script the instructions refer to.

Cam. 2 M/s Tom. Desk A.	TOM./ The villagers of Hogmorden are justly proud of the fact that three times in the past five years they have won 'The Best Kept Village' award.
Slide HOGMORDEN	/Thousands of tourists make their way there during the summer and clearing up after them became a major task.
Cam. 2 Tom A/B	/So for the past four years retired blacksmith seventy-year-old Tom Jennings made it his responsibility to keep the village streets clean and tidy.
Slide TOM	Sadly,/ Tom died last week, and there seemed no likely candidate to replace
Cam. 2 Tom A/B	him./ That was until yesterday, when a volunteer stepped forward to keep the reputation of the village intact. It was, would you believe, Tom's *elder brother*, Jack.
Mix to ENG	Here's Harriet./ ENG. ROAD SWEEPER. Running time: 3′ 46″ Super. 'Jack Jennings' at 22″ Out words: '. . . I think I'm good for another eighty years. . . .
Mix Cam. 3 C/U Dick	(laughter)./

The director marks on the scripts only those instructions and abbreviations which relate to *his* involvement in the programme. 'M/s Tom' simply means mid-shot of Tom. 'Tom A/B' stand for Tom as before, in other words in the same shot of Tom which the camera offered earlier. 'Super Jack Jennings at 22″', of course, tells him that at twenty-two seconds into the film he must instruct the vision mixer to superimpose Jack's name over a shot of him on the ENG report. The 'out words' are obviously the final words in the ENG story, and on hearing these, which should occur three minutes and forty-six seconds from the start of the report, the director will call for a mix to camera three for the next item in the programme.

The director's eyes shift swiftly from his script to the bank of monitors in front of him and back again to the script. Programmes like these use many visual sources. There are three or four cameras to choose from at any time; perhaps two machines supplying film sequences, another two providing the ENG pictures; maybe a camera shot from a studio hundred of miles away where an MP (unable to make the long journey from London in time) waits to be interviewed later in the programme via a monitor in the main studio.

Every one of these incoming sources, as they are termed, has a monitor allocated to it. When a director wants to tell his vision mixer to cut to a scheduled close-up on camera three, he (and she) needs to confirm that camera three is in fact on the close-up and not still on the caption or map which has been transmitted minutes ago and no longer required. Each time that the director calls out the next shot required, his eyes swing to the monitor concerned, checking that the shot is ready and to his liking.

Alongside him the vision mixer does the same, for she is trained to cut to a shot only when it is ready to be taken . . . an embarrassed pause waiting for a camera to complete a very fast move is preferable to cutting to a moving picture of the studio floor, followed by the hurried framing and focusing on a bewildered and embarrassed newsreader.

On live programmes like these the vision mixer, always an important person, carries much responsibility. Although many shots and sequences are scripted, as we have seen, other parts of the programme, such as interviews, are not. The successful coverage of these items depends very much on the speed and ability of the vision mixer to respond to the director's unrehearsed instructions.

The vision mixer marks her script with her own shorthand. To her, every source in a programme is identified by the button she must press in order to put it on the screen. She would not write 'slide' or 'ENG' on her script then, but simply 7 and 11, which are the buttons those sources are connected to on the panel before her. Her job demands many qualities; manual dexterity, speed of thought, the ability to remain calm at all times, self-confidence and that difficult-to-describe 'feel' for the job. It is she who punches the buttons on the impressive panel of buttons, knobs and levers in front of her, albeit to the director's instructions. Using the benefits of years of technological development, she can employ electronic 'wipes' as a transition from one shot to another.

In its simplest form a vertical line moves across the screen from left to right wiping out the existing shot as it moves and gradually replacing it with the new shot which is revealed behind the moving line. In practice there are dozens and dozens of variations as one evening's viewing will reveal. Although these effects are normally used on light entertainment and musical shows, they are occasionally utilised on the kind of live magazine programme we are looking at, particularly as a slick transition from one news film to another giving the programme a feeling of urgency in the process. Modern technology has now almost relegated the standard wipes to the realms of archaism, but care and skill are still needed in order to utilise them effectively.

A good vision mixer gives a director immense confidence, for he knows not only can she be relied upon to cut, mix or wipe to the right

The vision control engineer (left), the lighting director and the console operator at work at their controls.

shot at exactly the right time, but also her speed of thought and lightning reactions will enable him to present the unscripted portions of the programme in a neat, competent manner. When things go wrong, as they often do, she can be relied upon to keep her head, follow his lead, and help extricate the programme from disaster with the minimum of fuss.

The vision mixer sits directly to one side of the director. On his other side sits the girl whose contribution is as vital to the success of the programme as anyone's, the PA. Although each individual television company has its own system, generally speaking her duties are clear cut. Using one stopwatch she keeps an eye on the overall timing of the programme, being able to tell the producer at any moment whether or not the programme is keeping to time, and if not by how much it is over- or under-running. For although items have been timed beforehand, presenters and newsreaders do sometimes deliver their lines at a different pace when on air. In addition, it is not always possible to bring an interview to a close exactly three minutes and thirty seconds after it started – the time allowed for it, perhaps, in the producer's calculations. It always seems that an interviewee launches into a long-winded answer just about the time when the PA is saying 'ten seconds left on interview' and the director is yelling to the interviewer to 'wrap it up'.

Using another stopwatch she times each individual item (such as an interview or a film) so that everyone knows when it will end and the next one commence. This information is particularly vital to both the producer and the director. If an interview seriously over-runs (say forty-five seconds or more) then the producer must decide what to drop from the programme later if it is to run to time – which it must. The director also needs to know how long an interview still has to run, for at some stage towards the end of it (about thirty seconds, usually) he will almost certainly have to peel one camera away from the interview to move to the presenter who will read the next link.

These programmes utilise both film and video contributions as we have seen. Although practice varies between companies, the machines carrying video tapes must be started five seconds before the pictures can be punched into the programme by the vision mixer; this enables them to get up to speed and for the sound and vision elements to stabilise themselves. So when ENG is scripted to follow a link, the ENG machine is cued to start rolling five seconds before the end of that link, and it is usually the PA's responsibility to do this, counting the seconds remaining before the ENG is available.

PA	*Presenter*
	So, for the past four years retired
	blacksmith, seventy-year-old Tom Jennings,
Stand by ENG	made it his responsibility to keep the
	village streets clean and tidy. Sadly,
	Tom died last week, and there seemed no
	likely candidate to replace him. That
	was until yesterday, when a volunteer
ENG ROLL!*	stepped forward to keep the reputation*
FOUR,* THREE,*	of the village* intact. It was,*
TWO,* ONE,*	would you believe,* Tom's *elder brother*,*
ZERO*	Jack. Here's Harriet.*

At zero the first shot of the tape is visible and the vision mixer can cut or mix to it.

It is almost universal practice on this type of programme for the presenters and newsreaders to wear a tiny earpiece through which they can hear all that is happening in the control room – the director's instructions, the PA's cues to film and video tape machine operators, and the many timings she continuously calls. The presenters can also hear the producer if needed, extremely useful if the producer wants to extend or reduce the length of an interview while on air, or if he wants to change the order of items still to come in the programme.

It is a source of bewilderment to many people that a presenter can continue to look calmly into the camera lens and read his script without faltering while all bedlam is going on in his ear. Although most presenters have the benefit of a device which projects the words

The back-room boys – telecine in action.

of his script, via mirrors, onto the camera lens enabling him to look straight at the viewer while speaking his lines, nevertheless he could be forgiven if the sounds in his earpiece distract him from what he is saying.

In practice, presenters seem to master the skill of listening to one thing while saying another fairly quickly, and, having done so, wonder how they ever managed without the ever-present earpiece. Without it they feel isolated, out of touch with what is happening in the control room. With it, they can hear things starting to go wrong and begin to anticipate what their function will be to correct this.

As an example: when the PA cues the ENG machine operator to roll he usually does so immediately, and she can then count the seconds to when it will be available to be punched into the programme. Sometimes this does not happen. There might be a temporary malfunction of the electronic communication system between the PA and the operator ('talk-back', as it is called). It might be that the operator was distracted just at the very second the PA called her cue. Perhaps he pressed the button to start his machine rolling and, for no apparent reason, it did not respond.

Whatever the cause, if there is a delay of, say, two seconds before the machine starts, the presenter (hearing all this in his earpiece) knows he will have to extend his link into the ENG item by those two extra seconds. Since he is coming to the end of his link, as we explained earlier, he must decide instantly whether he will add another six words

Tension in the control room.

to his link, or slow down the pace of his delivery. Whatever he does must look natural if the viewer is to be unaware of what is happening. That comes with experience. That little earpiece nevertheless gives the presenter a couple of vital seconds' warning of what is needed from him.

That is a simple example, of course, and in practice presenters must cope with greater disasters than the one we looked at. Sometimes through human error ENGs appear in the wrong order, and a light-hearted link into the tape of the eighty-year-old roadsweeper is followed, not by the item on him, but by a video of the funeral of a soldier killed in Belfast. This kind of intensely embarrassing error does creep into live programmes, especially when items are loaded in a hurry and under pressure minutes before the programme is due to be transmitted.

In the control room it is often four or five seconds before the error is noted. This is not due to negligence, but by the very nature of people's responsibilities. The PA, having cued the ENG to roll and counted the seconds to zero, starts her second watch to time the item immediately she hears the director instruct the vision mixer to cut to the tape. The PA has no time to look at the pictures: her head is buried in her script and her eyes glance at her stopwatch as she calls out the information which would be useful if the right item were on the screen: 'Five seconds to supering the first name . . . four three two one zero . . . one minute fifteen on tape . . . ten seconds to Tom "voice over" . . . nine, eight, seven. . . .'

The director, having seen the first frame of ENG appear on the monitor, tells the vision mixer to cut to it and immediately busies himself with what must happen next: 'Stand by for the first name super . . . take it . . . lose it . . . stand by, Tom . . . camera three clear to Harry. . . .'

The vision mixer, too, having checked that there is a picture for her to cut to, does just that and then turns to her next task, that of superimposing Jack Jennings' name. Her hands move instinctively to the correct buttons and levers, she glances at her script for reassurance, she concentrates on the PA counting the seconds, and awaits the director's next instruction.

So it is usually someone like the producer or technical supervisor who notices that the wrong item is being transmitted, and that, too, takes time to be realised. The opening shot might be a wide shot of a street with a slow pan to the street name; nothing to raise any suspicions that we might not be looking at the street sweeper film. It may take two more shots before the dreadful realisation emerges that we are, in fact, looking at a funeral. Once this is realised no time must be lost to cut away from the film to a presenter, in this case Dick, and to get him to apologise and lead into the next item when the producer and director can then discuss how they can put the programme back on course.

It is not always possible to cut to a specific presenter just like that. One camera might still be on its way across the studio to another presenter. The others might be pointing at maps, or objects to be seen in the next item, or on interviewees who are later to be interviewed. Through his earpiece Dick has heard the drama and anticipates his coming role in the rescue act. He hears the director's tense instructions: 'as fast as you can camera three . . . hold it . . . take it, cue Harry.' Harry's calm face replaces the wrong story . . . 'I'm sorry about that . . . we seemed to have lost our roadsweeper for the moment . . . we'll try and get him back for a little later. But now . . . here's Harriet.' Harriet links into an interview. The director manipulates his shots, and the vision mixer cuts from one to another as he instructs her. The PA keeps a check on the timing of the item so that Harriet can keep it to the planned length.

Even as this is happening the producer and director confer. An item which should have appeared and run for three minutes and forty-six seconds did not appear where expected. Can it appear later on in the programme or has it in fact been accidentally left out of the pile of ENG tapes altogether? Is there time to check the remaining tapes to see if it is there? In any event, there are over three-and-a-half minutes of the programme which might never appear if the tape is not there . . .

so how best can they fill that gap? So it goes on throughout the interview.

Although no-one likes to be associated with that kind of embarrassing error, there is no doubt that the possibility that it can happen at any time adds to the adrenalin output of those engaged on this type of live programme.

There is little in television to compare with the thrill of 'going live'. It begins in earnest with the final countdown into the programme when the tension in the control room is so vivid that it can sometimes terrify visitors who are privileged to be allowed to witness the scene. It continues throughout the programme, for everyone knows that there can be no lapse in concentration; no forgetting that disaster can strike at any time which will call for quick reflexes, lightning decisions and firm judgement.

As the closing music swells up, the 'end credits' roll through the screen and the PA counts the seconds to the end of the programme; even at this stage no-one relaxes, for things can still go wrong and mar an otherwise perfect programme. 'Ten seconds to off air . . . nine . . . eight . . . seven . . . six. . . .' The director's voice cuts across her: 'Mix to end slide.' Alongside him the vision mixer makes the last of many dozens of cuts, mixes and wipes she has performed throughout the programme, a large number unscripted and unrehearsed.

'Three to off air . . . two . . . one . . . zero.' The final shot of the programme is faded out and replaced by whatever has been scheduled to follow it. The programme is over; the studio is off the air. There is an immediate release of tension, almost as if fifty people have been holding their breath for half-an-hour. Everyone talks at once as a heady satisfaction takes over. 'Well done studio . . . thanks, Bill . . . well done, love . . . terrific.' Tomorrow's programme is light years away; right now everyone is on their own private 'high' and many find it difficult, if not impossible, to just climb into their cars and drive away. So they tend to congregate, over a drink perhaps or back in their open-plan office, and relive the exciting parts of the programme, the places where it might have ground to a standstill, the success or otherwise of an item, the balance of an interview, or the cause of the wrong ENG appearing where it should not.

Tomorrow, another piece of blank paper waits to be filled. Another programme which will be totally different to tonight's. A new set of challenges, problems, pitfalls and perhaps another success to celebrate.

Live programmes may not have the polish of recorded shows where mistakes can be wiped clean and errors eliminated. 'Going live', however, is really what separates television from the film industry. It is what television was all about until the invention of the video tape. The very immediacy of this visual medium outstrips all others when programmes are transmitted live, and live television gives those who are involved the unique excitement and job satisfaction which can rarely be found elsewhere.

Although a successful live programme can bring a peak of euphoria, there is an equal trough of despondency when the programme has gone badly. No second chance to do anything, no retakes, no going back and inserting the right item where the wrong one appeared. The very ingredients which give live programmes their thrill bring frustration and despair when things go wrong. It can be very disheartening when an item which has taken many people all day to prepare is ruined during transmission by someone's error, by equipment failure or by lack of concentration. The director is well aware of how much effort has gone into the stories in the programme; items which he is ultimately responsible for presenting on the television screen. A major item can contain film and video sequences, perhaps slides and still photographs, maybe two or three presenters and certainly pages of carefully written script. One simple error, like the funeral incident we looked at earlier, can start a chain-reaction of incidents which might well lead to the item simply falling to pieces, leaving the viewer baffled, the producer furious, and the director suicidal, whether it was his fault or not.

So live programming is not all highs, far from it; but it is to the credit of those who work on these programmes that so few major mistakes are noticed by the viewer. To be successful on live programmes those involved, especially those in the control rooms, must really be so much on top of their job that it is instinctive. In addition they must be capable of remaining cool and objective whatever is happening, and have the ability to make fast decisions which are the right ones in the particular circumstances.

Before leaving live programmes there is one comparable area worth looking at which is vital to the smooth running of a television company's output, yet it attracts little publicity and the average viewer is totally unaware of its existence.

Let us take a look at a typical hour's viewing one evening on ITV. The local news magazine we have just studied comes to an end. The last shot fades away exactly on the second it was scheduled to. Up comes a commercial advertisement for a brand of coffee (on video tape, say) followed by a commercial for a well-known car tyre. More commercials follow, including one which consists of a number of slides with an announcer somewhere in the building reading the script which has been written by the advertisers.

Finally a caption appears detailing the programmes which can be seen during the rest of the evening, again with our announcer telling us what delights await us. This fades away and is replaced by the opening title sequence for *Coronation Street*. The interlude between the end of the local magazine programme and the beginning of the soap opera has been two minutes and five seconds. Two minutes and five seconds packed with visual material from a variety of sources – film, tape, slides with live commentary and so on.

Someone has to punch those sources onto the screen, or, to be more exact, has to relay those sources to the transmitter which will beam them into the atmosphere where they can be picked up by the domestic television aerial and be selected for viewing onto the home television set. Someone has to cue the film and video machines to roll five seconds before they are needed. That same someone has to show us the opening titles of *Coronation Street* exactly two minutes and five seconds after the end of the live local programme, because that is the length that this commercial break has been scheduled to last.

The man responsible for this important task is called a transmission controller, and he is responsible for ensuring that the right pictures and sound reach your screens exactly when they should. At the appointed time the transmission controller will fade that studio off the air and busy himself with filling the commercial break with the scheduled material – the advertisements which keep his company breathing. Until recently some of these commercials were on film, others on video tape or on video cartridges or cassettes. Nowadays it is common practice to transfer all commercials (film or video) onto separate cartridges. By the extensive use of computers these 'carts' can be located and placed in the correct order for each commercial break in a very short space of time.

At the end of the commercial break he will, in common with his counterparts in all the other ITV companies, fade out the last commercial and fade up the opening shot of *Coronation Street* i.e. the Granada station symbol. *Coronation Street*, however, is transmitted by Granada Television from its Manchester studios. Not only must the Transmission Controller in Granada roll the video tape and present it to all the other companies exactly at that second, but each transmission controller in every company must also have that 'feed' from Manchester connected to a button on his panel. Without this facility he could not send Granada's programme to his own transmitter, and therefore the viewers in his company's area.

Throughout a day's transmission the transmission controller needs a variety and changeable number of feeds on his panel, for programmes will emanate from companies other than Granada. Master control engineers, as they are called, arrange for all those feeds from other companies to be made available to the transmission controller as and when required. They are also responsible for more technical matters which are beyond the scope of this book, but they are vital back-room operators without whose expertise no company could function.

Finally, let us consider the situation when a company (let us say London Weekend Television) is transmitting a live programme which is being fed to all the other ITV companies. During this programme there is to be a commercial break to be taken somewhere around the mid-way point of its scheduled running time. It is a discussion programme, say, and it is, therefore, almost impossible for London Weekend to be precise to the second as to when part one of the programme will end. A discussion might be going so well that the producer will want it to continue a few minutes more than scheduled, rather than interrupt it with an immovable commercial break.

That is all very well for the producer at LWT. Throughout the ITV network, however, each transmission controller needs to know when 'part one' of the programme is eventually going to end, because exactly five seconds before that happens he must roll his video or film machines which carry the first of his company's commercials. Each company puts out its own commercials, and so fifteen transmission controllers throughout the country must simultaneously roll their first commercials five seconds before the end of part one.

How is this done? Very simply. When the LWT producer feels that the interview is running out of steam he declares that it is about time for the commercial break. The PA then flicks a special switch which puts a tiny symbol (called a 'cue dot') onto the top right-hand corner of the picture. This is usually a small square with diagonal lines inside, and it tells all transmission controllers around the network that part one of the programme has about a minute to run.

Fifty-five seconds later, as the vision mixer at LWT mixes to the 'end of part one' caption (which is always left up for at least five seconds) the PA switches off the cue dot. This tells all the waiting transmission controllers that 'part one' of the programme has just five seconds to run, and they know that they can then set in motion the wheels which five seconds later will provide the commercials to fill the scheduled time slot and which are so vital to the economy of each individual company.

10 OUTSIDE BROADCASTS

Live programmes, as we have seen, underline the differences between the film industry and television, for nothing the film industry can do can match the immediacy of live television especially in the area of factual programmes. The coming of television spelt the end for Pathé and Gaumont British News, much loved by cinema-goers. Viewers became accustomed to seeing newsworthy items within hours of their occurrence, not days, and with the live outside broadcast (or OB) the viewer was presented with the ultimate in armchair viewing: events from anywhere in the world brought to him as they took place.

This facility of the OB to go to where the action is and capture it as it happens is surely one of the most exciting and spectacular features of the television medium. For sports lovers in particular, television brought their dreams to reality and have continued to do so ever since. Not so many years ago it would have been laughable to suggest that a family sitting at home in England could watch the Olympic Games in Tokyo as they were actually taking place. Add the bonus of informed comment, instantaneous slow-motion replays, face-to-face interviews with the famous and the failures, and a sophisticated presentation bringing live coverage from a variety of sports taking place in a dozen different locations sometimes hundreds of miles apart, then the impact of the live OB cannot be denied. The viewer sees more than the spectactor.

It is true that much is now taken for granted, yet the viewer's enthusiasm is still as great as ever. He has become much more discerning and less easily pleased with the mediocre, and no major sport can now function and pretend that television does not exist. So deals have been negotiated between sporting bodies and the media in an attempt to satisfy an insatiable TV public which now feels it has a right to watch live coverage of Wimbledon, the FA Cup Final, cricket test matches, rugby internationals, motor racing grands prix, major athletics meetings (including the European, Commonwealth and Olympic Games, not forgetting the Winter Olympics) and dozens and dozens more.

A list of all live sporting OBs shown on BBC and ITV in the course of a year would stagger the average viewer, and we have not even looked at the events which were covered 'as live' and later edited to provide the best highlights often within an hour of the event taking place. So there can be little doubt that it is in the arena of sport that the

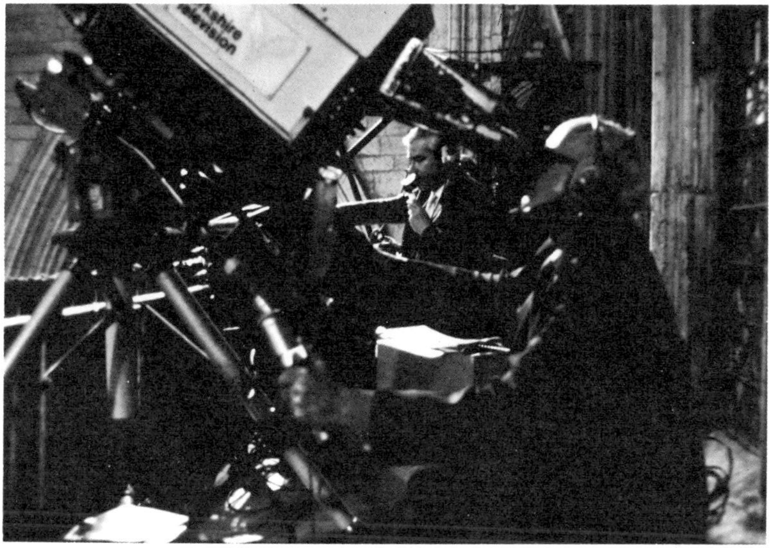

An OB cameraman and commentator (Alistair Burnet).

television OB reigns supreme. It is not without its detractors, and many people feel that it ultimately acts to the detriment of sport, or that it causes changes within sport which are artificially brought about to satisfy the demands of the television medium.

Nevertheless, television has brought comparatively little-known or rarely-watched sports to the foreground, and helped the participants to reach superstar proportions. Large numbers of viewers means sponsorship by major firms eager to see their product advertised in front of the viewing public as often as possible. So they pour in the money for big prizes, the behind-the-scenes organisation takes on a new gloss, and co-operation with the media is absolute. What was once the bar-room game of darts with a cloth cap image is now a well-oiled television entertainment machine which rolls around the world. The skill of the players is breathtaking. It always was; but now they are regularly watched by millions, and this is reflected in the mode of dress, their front-of-camera behaviour. The pressures from other competitors is relentless, but the rewards are staggering.

Snooker, the so-called sign of a wasted youth, is now not only extremely respectable but also compulsive viewing for millions of people who have never been in a snooker hall in their lives.

There is, however, another side to the coin. England's national game, football, has suffered a television decline. There are a number of reasons for this. Many people feel that television has provided saturation coverage over the years, and that the viewer has become immune to the basic lure of the game. The game itself has its own troubles with crowd violence, falling gates, and behaviour on the field which often irritates and angers. England's national team can have little to shout about, and many feel that the quality of play on the field, with few exceptions, is not worth switching on to view. Perhaps television has added to the game's headaches by exposing, under the slow-motion microscope and the tongue of the commentator, the weaknesses and cynicisms which the viewer no longer wishes to tolerate.

Whatever the arguments for and against the merits of live television coverage of sport, there is no doubt that it is here to stay. The viewer has become so accustomed, as well, to the sophisticated coverage which television provides that he can be extremely critical of standards. It is no longer sufficient for a television company merely to take its cameras to a sporting event to ensure that it will have a captive television audience. It now matters very much indeed just how skilfully and imaginatively the production team presents the event to the viewer.

Yet for many years that kind of complacency was rife in British television. Year after year the same three or four cameras found their way to the same points around a sporting venue which they had always occupied. The coverage of soccer matches, for example, became predicatable but safe. Slow-motion replays during the course of play were unthinkable and the entertainment on the screen was only marginally better than taking the trouble to actually go to the match itself.

It is generally recognised in the industry that Bob Gardam, an imaginative and determined director, was the first in this country to bring a new, more vivid dimension to the coverage of football. He was not afraid to place his cameras in unconventional positions, such as low down just behind the goalmouth, and he also urged his cameramen to zoom into the big close-ups of the players at the moments of triumphs and despair which is now universal practice. One of his innovative camera placings at Wembley Stadium is known to this day as Gardam's Pit, and there is no doubt that his style brought new excitement to television coverage of the game.

Another jolt for those in live OBs occurred with the import of video tapes of American television coverage of its major sports, such as their grid-iron football. Television professionals and viewers alike could not fail to be impressed by the slick use of a multitude of cameras and slow-motion techniques. Nothing which happens in this most complex of games happens without one camera at least covering it in revealing detail. Major incidents are replayed instantly and from a variety of camera positions. The commentary is relaxed and informative, and there is constant superimposition of facts and figures brilliant in its layout and mass of information, and this in a game obsessed with statistics.

Even more surprising was the effect on the coverage of the game we thought we could present better than anyone in the world – cricket. Over the years the BBC, in particular, seemed unbeatable in the manner of their presentation, and there was little to complain of until Australian television coverage of the 1982–83 series 'down under' showed us televised cricket in a more exciting and informative way than we had ever seen. Any incident around the wicket was immediately played back from a variety of angles, no catches were missed, the close-ups gave us new insights into the subtleties of the game, and once again the graphics superimposed at strategic times began to rival those of the Americans and their grid-iron football television coverage. Where we had settled for four or five cameras to cover a game the Australians demanded at least nine. True, it is much more expensive to increase the television hardware and personnel to this level, not forgetting the extra number of slow-motion facilities to be allotted to each camera to provide this multiplicity of coverage. Nevertheless, the viewer has seen what can be done and now looks for the same coverage from British television. Televised cricket has never been the same since.

The effect of this search for improved television coverage has revealed itself in many ways in a variety of sports. Just compare present-day coverage of football or tennis with the presentation of ten or fifteen years ago. The more polished and informative style of commentary, the improved use of sound, and above all the more adventurous and skilful placing of cameras which offer a greater variety of shots and which take the viewer right into the midst of the action; all these combine to serve the viewer with superb live sporting action.

The basis for all good OB coverage is the correct placing of cameras and the right choice of lenses. Unless the cameras can cover virtually anything which might happen during a sporting event, superb commentary and slick graphics will not prevent the discerning viewer from tearing his hair out in frustration if he continually misses what he wants to see. Over the years, the OB director has become adept at this important art of placing his cameras to the best advantage. The director does not have an unlimited number of cameras available for an OB. If he is using one scanner to cover a football match, for example, that scanner might not be able to accept the input of more than five cameras. It might be that his company has just that one scanner available for his OB and he must settle for this five-camera coverage.

He approaches the decision of where to place these cameras firstly in a logical manner. One camera must be placed high and on the centre line to present the main 'cover shot'. This camera shows the viewer the general view of the action as would be seen by a spectator at the match sitting centrally and well up in the grandstand. It shows the general pattern of play, and the movement and tactics of attackers and defenders alike as the ball is passed, kicked or dribbled towards one goal or another.

He usually places alongside that camera a second which will concentrate on following the man with the ball, just wide enough to include any nearby opponents giving the viewer good close-up action of tackles or skilful ball-play. Because, like the first camera, this too is mounted high in the grandstand no-one can get in the way of its shots, so it presents good, uninterrupted, close-up action.

The director usually places the third camera roughly at ground level and as near to the centre line as possible. This is the camera which gives us those exciting, revealing close-ups of the players which we have come to expect from the better type of OB coverage. The cameraman on this camera must really be an accomplished operator and remain extremely alert throughout the game. For much of his time he will be fighting to keep his subjects framed correctly and in focus despite the fact that they are moving quickly and mercurially in every direction. The faster he can find the scorer of the goal and focus on him the sooner the director can cut to his camera for that jubilant leap, that smile, that defiant victory gesture which is the trademark of the ecstatic scorer.

Cameramen who operate this camera have become extremely adept at the skills involved. Just watch a televised match and note how amazingly quickly the director is able to present just the close-up needed on just the right player following an incident: the writhing of the apparently injured player, the protestation of innocence, the unheard reprimand of the referee, the bowed head of the beaten goalkeeper, the manager in the dug-out screaming at his players, the substitute warming up. These are now all part of the television coverage we have become accustomed to, and they have certainly brought a vivid, exciting and revealing dimension to our appreciation of the game. The players have not been slow, however, to catch on to the close-ups they can offer to this camera, and a certain amount of play-acting has crept into the game on television. That has surely been a small price to pay for the grass-roots spectacle provided.

Let us not forget the value of sound in all this. These cameras are usually mounted with highly directional microphones (gun mics) which point whichever way the camera points, and which bring us extremely close and intimate sound to augment the close action presented by the camera.

The director has two cameras left to place. From this point on it is very much a matter of personal preference between one director and another. Some like to place a high camera behind each of the goals, sometimes linking each to its own video machine so that instant slow-motion replays can be available from a completely new angle of view. These interesting angles often give a completely new flavour to a spectacular goal or save, and often show incidents which were not apparent to the centrally placed cameras. They are particularly useful, for example, in spotting a ball which has been deflected *en route* to goal, impossible to spot sometimes from the grandstand.

Some directors settle for one high camera behind one goal and the fifth place very low behind the other goal. The shots from this low camera almost take the viewer into the goalmouth – and can be tremendously dramatic on such occasions as corner kicks, or on replays of penalty kicks. Other directors prefer to have one camera 'hand held', allowing the cameraman to wander around the fringes of the pitch, giving him even greater options in his camera coverage. Much depends, of course, on the actual layout of the football ground itself. The more modern grandstands have excellent facilities for television coverage, with ample room for cameras, commentators, monitors and tables. On older grounds the director often has to order special scaffolding to be built, or utilise one of the types of flexible hoists mounted on the back of a special lorry.

The director also decides on the best placing of microphones to give him the close sound which brings his pictures to life. In addition the commentator needs a microphone, of course, which is usually a 'lip mic' which he holds close to his mouth so that his commentary is not drowned by the roar of the crowd around him. He also wears 'cans', listening to the director constantly throughout the game so that he knows which camera and which shot the director is about to take. This way they work in harmony.

Sir Alistair Burnet, ITV's top big occasion commentator, in action with a lip mic.

In front of him the commentator has a monitor showing him which shots the director is showing the viewer at all times, and he also has his own sheaf of notes spread before him. These sheets are crammed with information which has taken him many, many hours of diligent research to accumulate. Over the years the top commentators gather a wealth of material on virtually every player in the football league, continually updating this as players change clubs, break new scoring records, or gain further honours in the game.

We are accustomed to hearing such facts as 'and that's the first goal Shilton has conceded in six European Cup games', or 'that was the goal Arsenal needed to be safe from relegation, and it took an eighteen year-old in only his third first-team game to score it'. Commentaries are riddled with facts and background colour which can only enhance our interest in the game, and perhaps help us understand it better, or appreciate the human dramas enacted before us. The commentator is solely responsible for amassing these facts and figures, and he must know where to find the relevant ones throughout the game while still keeping up his commentary. He cannot be expected to know all the facts about a substitute who has just run onto the field but he must find it fast, for the viewer wants to know as much about the new player as possible, and immediately.

The director sitting in the confines of the scanner has no easy task. It is customary on such fast-moving OBs as football for the director to do his own vision mixing, i.e. he actually punches the buttons and moves the levers on the vision mixing panel which send the pictures out to the viewer. It has been proved quicker for the director to do this than pass his instructions on to a vision mixer sitting alongside him. That extra responsibility, however, means that the director must really be alert throughout the transmission, for he talks continuously to his cameramen, telling first one to zoom out to reveal some incident, then another to find the goalscorer – fast! All the while he listens to the commentator so that anything important which he says can be backed up by the appropriate picture. It is maddening to sit at home and hear the commentator describe the ecstatic convulsions of a sixteen-year-old who has scored a goal on his first-team debut while the director shows us a shot of the spectators.

The game of football moves so fast, certainly for the director who has so much to do and so much to react to, that it is vital for him to brief his cameras thoroughly beforehand as to what he expects from them in any given situation. It is hopeless if at a corner kick all five cameras offer a shot of the corner kicker. So every cameraman must know what exactly his function is.

This the director establishes while looking at his shots before the game. He takes each cameraman through his duties one by one. 'Camera one zoom out to include the centre circle. That is your normal cover-shot, if you have to zoom out to cover the action get back to that size when you can. Once you've panned to include the goalmouth, keep it on the edge of your frame and tighten with the action. On corners give me a loose shot in the goal area . . .' and so on. 'Camera three, I want good close-up stuff on you. Any player who does anything or has anything done to him . . . I want . . . fast! On corner kicks give me the kicker then find the guy who shoots or scores . . . fast.' The director goes through each camera like this, leaving no doubt in the cameraman's mind what his function is. The director for his part knows that if the cameramen follow his instructions he can cut from camera to camera on a corner, for example, almost without checking the camera shots on the monitors in front of him. He *knows* that camera number one is giving a general view in the goal area, that camera number two is concentrating on the closer shots around the goalkeeper, that camera number three is on the corner-kicker, that camera number four is offering his worm's-eye-view from behind the right-hand post, and so on.

Of course, in practice, a crew becomes accustomed to working with the same two or three OB directors and are familiar with their individual methods of covering matches. This pre-match briefing is an essential reminder, if nothing else, of how this particular director wants things done. For freelance directors who move from company to company it is vital that his crews know what is expected of them from a man they have never worked with before.

Although studio television cameramen do go out on OBs, and in some companies all cameramen take turns at OBs, those cameramen who spend their entire lives on OBs, and might have done so for well over a decade, are somehow a race apart from their studio counterparts. Following a group of horses racing for the finishing line, or singling out a player who has just scored a goal, requires a different *feel* to camerawork than that needed to zoom in delicately to a close-up of a rose at the end of a beautiful love song in the controlled situation of the studio. It is not more or less skilful, it is simply different. There is no doubt that the good OB cameraman does develop an amazing ability to find the right shot at the right time and do the right thing with it.

It becomes instinctive to these cameramen to follow the flight of a well-struck golf ball, to hold focus on a racing car at 150 miles an hour, to find the football player the director wants even before he asks for it, to keep the tennis ball in shot without undue camera movement, to follow the cricket ball as it races for the boundary, to know when the ball is going to break from the rugby scrum and to go with it.

They are used to working at great distances from the scanner, on high scaffolding and 140-foot flexible mountings. They accept whatever the weather will throw at them, and learn to function effectively no matter how cold or wet or windy. They are familiar with cramped and uncomfortable locations, of rigging their equipment into all kinds of awkward places in filthy weather. They are adept at compromising

OB cameras set up to cover a race meeting.

between the required and the impossible. Not for them the facilities of the studio where cameras can be connected to specified sockets around the wall, and where they can place their cameras on special pedestals which glide noiselessly and effortlessly around the smooth, billiard-table-like surface of the studio floor. On OBs the camera cables are hauled by riggers across fields and over roads to where the cameras are. Cameras are winched up to the top of scaffolds or onto high roofs.

In fact, OBs are rather unglamorous. The scanner, the mobile video tape recording vehicle, the ancillary trucks, vans and cars are seemingly dotted haphazardly in a confined, usually muddy enclave. Cables spew from these vehicles in all manner of directions, some snaking into buildings, others carried across roads and roofs and fields to the cameras, microphones and monitors dotted around the location. OBs are all about compromise, because no two locations are alike, and no location can possibly offer the cosy sophistication of the purpose-built studio.

The lamps which the lighting director needs on indoor OB locations cannot be mounted from the pre-constructed, integrated grids available to his studio counterpart. More often than not he must order special scaffolding to be constructed to carry the bars from which his lamps can be hung. On such OBs as horse-racing the distances from cameras to scanner can be vast, and hundreds of yards of cables are dragged across inhospitable ground to where they are hoisted up to specially-built camera towers and connected to cameras which themselves have to be transported and lifted into place. Cables, too, for microphones and monitors, must be laid, connected and tested. Inevitably, the complicated and delicate equipment reacts to the constant disruption and manhandling. Always on OBs there are technical breakdowns, problems, cameras which give electronic headaches, microphones which malfunction, communications which break down. The comparison between OBs and studio operations is akin to that between deep-sea fishing and match angling. There is nothing subtle about rigging and operating OBs.

Yet there is little to compare with the satisfaction which comes from arriving at a location, overcoming its limitations, getting the equipment to work, and beaming the programme back to base from where it is fed to the waiting millions at home.

Pictures and sound from an OB, of course, count for nothing if they cannot be fed to where they can be transmitted to the viewer. In the weeks and months before an OB takes place, the links engineers visit the location and determine how the output from the site can be routed back to the transmitter. Usually this involves beaming the pictures to a high point where they are received and beamed to another, and maybe another, until they are picked up by the studio or transmitter.

The viewer is unaware that his enjoyment of a major sporting or spectacular event is made possible not just by the people who have humped the equipment into place, brought the electronic complexity to life, directed and commentated on the event and covered the action with brilliant camerawork. More importantly he is indebted to nameless, unsung men who sit cold and lonely in isolated farmyards or on icy, windswept hill-tops, operating the equipment which picks up the television signals from the OB. They maintain the quality and strength of these signals before beaming them on to the next lonely links engineer.

Establishing these links between one high point and another is a skill built up over many years, as one links engineer learnt to his cost. He confirmed that there would be no problems in beaming a signal from point A to point B. The one could be seen from the other, therefore television contact could be guaranteed. The links were set up. When the OB went on air to bring the viewers coverage of an important football match, all was well. As the match progressed, however, the pictures became gradually weaker (as did the sound) until they eventually vanished altogether. There followed the usual fury and inquest which is inseparable from failure in television.

The explanation emerged. What the links engineer had not noticed when making his investigation was that between points A and B the local Gas Board premises were sited. As luck would have it, during the course of the televised football match the gasometer, as it is commonly known, became filled with gas, rising higher and higher as it did so.

Slowly but surely it severed the television connection between the OB and the next link in the transmission chain. It was a mistake that the links engineer never, ever repeated, and illustrates a lesson in OB coverage which underlines the importance of the back-room boys whose existence is largely unknown even to many of those who work in television.

We mentioned lenses briefly earlier, and the choice of which lens to place on which camera is vital to the success of an OB. The development of good, reliable zoom lenses with a variety of ranges transformed OBs. When cameras were fitted with lenses of fixed angles of view (even though there might be a choice of four mounted on a rotatable turret), the coverage they were able to provide was extremely limited compared to the vast options available with present-day zoom lenses.

Most zoom lenses used on OBs have a range from the widest to tightest angle of view to the ratio of 20:1, that means an angle of view of 50° at its widest and 2.5° at its tightest. Some zoom lenses offer a fantastic range of 40 : 1, and these are extremely useful to have when the camera is a great distance from the action and both wide and very close shots are needed. Picking the right lens for a camera is almost as important as picking the right position for it at a sporting venue. Putting the camera at the right height, too, is a critical decision for the director, for a change of height of only 10 feet or so can make an amazing difference to the range of shots the cameraman can offer to the director.

Picking the right height is something which comes with experience, for it is very difficult at first for a novice director to stand on a golf course and determine whether he needs a 40-foot or a 70-foot scaffold if the camera to be placed there is to give him the coverage he needs over five holes of a tournament. Since 70-foot scaffolds cost more to erect than 40-footers a mistake on his part can prove costly in more ways than one.

Techniques for covering the range of sporting events seen on television are constantly updated. As more sophisticated equipment becomes available, together with better lenses, lighter cameras, superior microphones, and improved electronic graphics, so directors and producers develop their style of presentation to utilise these technical assets to improve their television presentation of sporting OBs.

All this, however, puts a greater strain on the OB director. Take the basic coverage at a cricket match where the bowler runs up to bowl, the batsman hits it towards the boundary, a fielder chases and gathers the ball and throws it to the wicket-keeper as the batsmen scamper home for two runs. In its simplest form the director cuts to a very wide shot as the bowler runs up, showing the placing of fielders around the wicket. Just before the ball is bowled he mixes to the shot directly behind the bowler's arm, revealing just the bowler, batsman and wicket-keeper. As the batsman strikes the ball the director cuts to a wider shot, and this camera follows the ball as it is overhauled by the fielder. The director then cuts briefly to the shot showing how the batsman are running between the wickets, before cutting back to a close shot of the fielder picking up the ball and throwing it to the wicket-keeper. Another cut to the two batsmen haring for their second run, followed by a close shot of the wicket-keeper catching the ball and dislodging the bails virtually completes the sequence, with perhaps another close-up of the fielder as the spectators applaud his efforts.

Eight different, spontaneous shots in the space of say 12 seconds, and that sequence represents only the basic coverage. Watch modern-day presentation and note how techniques have advanced. In addition to the shots which made up that sequence the director now introduces further camera angles to give the action greater impact. A brief side view of the bowler's run-up; a close-up of the batsman's nervous shuffles as he waits for the ball; a quarter-size shot of the players running between wickets placed in a box to one side of the fielder chasing the ball; a close-up of the wicket-keeper's appeal followed by the umpire's studied indifference; shots of the fielder's disappointment and the batsmen's relief; a slow-motion replay of the incident first from the usual angle of view and then from a completely different viewpoint. All these shots *in addition* to the basic coverage give some idea of the quick thinking needed by director and cameramen alike.

This type of mental agility continues ball after ball, over after over, hour after hour. Let us not forget the graphics which constantly update the state of play, adding bowling figures, runs required to win, minutes and overs remaining and so on. Little wonder that it is customary on this type of OB for a director to be relieved every few hours by a colleague.

Television coverage of any sport, if it is to be done well, demands this high level of concentration and reaction often over long periods. An afternoon spent in detailed study of sporting OBs will show just how much thought must have gone into the preparations beforehand, and will reveal just how quickly the director uses the shots available to him to provide his own style of coverage. Probably the most comprehensive coverage of sport is to be found in the USA where technology and techniques are brilliantly exploited. We in the UK can offer nothing to compare with the coverage of the annual Superbowl – the American Football Cup Final.

Obviously directors must learn the sports they are televising, for unless they do so they cannot show the interested viewer what he wants to see during any action sequence. The techniques of television coverage vary greatly from sport to sport. There is no comparison between the camera layouts on such OBs as horse racing, tennis, snooker and swimming; that is obvious, for each requires a vastly different approach, both in the preparation and the shooting. When

OB coverage of a majestic event.

we remember that the director is constantly searching for ways to improve this specialised presentation of television sport, it is clear that coverage is best left to directors and crews who are skilled in these types of programmes, and this is usually what happens in practice.

Of course not all OBs are live, nor do they only cover sporting venues. Virtually any event which happens outside the confines of the studio can be the target for an OB if the television company thinks there will be sufficient viewer interest. Flower shows, beauty contests, country fairs, military tattoos, variety shows; these and thousands more are familiar viewing throughout the year. As we saw earlier when looking at *Emmerdale Farm*, it is fairly common practice to use OBs for drama sequences.

Who can deny the value of OBs on such an occasion as the wedding of Prince Charles and Lady Diana Spencer? In order to cover the whole Royal pageant the BBC and ITV used around a hundred cameras dotted along the route of the procession and within Westminster Abbey. Preparation by both organisations was meticulous, and there was the added bonus, not always available on OBs, of a full scale rehearsal on the days before the event.

We touched briefly on the role of the commentator on OBs, and on the Royal Wedding they were faced with a marathon task. As usual they accumulated a mass of information to enable them not only to explain and inform as the action unfolded, but also to augment this with the background snippets, those little facts and figures which gave added colour to the enjoyment of the event.

On those occasions when both the BBC and ITV cover a major event, the growing use of VCRs (video cassette recorders) has made it possible for the viewer to compare the merits of the two organisations' coverage. Many viewers watched the Royal Wedding on one channel while recording the other channel's efforts for later viewing. In fact video cassettes of BBC's and ITV's coverage were soon in the shops, and the public's view of which organisation provided the better coverage could be measured in commercial terms. This competition which has been raging for over a quarter of a century can only be good for the viewer and for television in general. Nothing stagnates like complacency, and stagnation is unthinkable when considering the role of the OB. A study of *Grandstand* or *World of Sport* over a long period should reveal whether television OB sports coverage is stagnating or not; the answer is that it certainly is not.

11 THE SPORTING MARATHONS

Although many sporting OBs are transmitted as single programmes in their own right, they are probably utilised most effectively on Saturday afternoons when both the BBC and ITV transmit their marathon sports presentations: *Grandstand* and *World of Sport* respectively. For four or five hours the viewer can relax in his own home and watch the best of the action from more than half-a-dozen sporting venues around the country. Events happening simultaneously are recorded and the highlights replayed later, while other contests are brought live into the living room. At each location the viewer has the benefit of multi-camera coverage, the best viewpoints, the biggest close-ups, informed commentary and opinion, slow-motion action replays, analysis, interviews with participants; all he misses is the sense of occasion which comes from actually being there.

In addition, the programmes are presented from studios which are geared to bring him the latest news and achievements from dozens of other sporting events. There are racing results, half-time and full-time football scores, live interviews, news items, nostalgic flashbacks, pictorial promises of events to come. Under the sure pilotage of the main 'anchor man' he is taken from the winners' enclosure at a major racecourse, to the world Badminton finals, to a half-time report on a first division football match, then to the heats and finals of a major swimming contest, back to the studio for more news and results, then motor cross, highlights of a world title fight, the latest situation in a golf tournament, the second half of a rugby league match, back to the studio yet again for more racing results and the full-time football scores as they pour in. The pattern is now familiar to sporting viewers, but the effort and professional involvement needed to mount and present the programmes is prodigious.

Both the BBC and ITV have more than two decades of experience in producing these marathon sporting efforts. They are both highly professional in their approach and commitment to the demands these programmes make on resources and abilities. The productions may differ in style and in the type of events they offer the viewer, but they do provide a splendid variety from which he can choose. Some events are exclusive to one programme or another; the BBC has a monopoly on rugby union internationals, for example. Often the decision to screen or not to screen an event is governed by considerations of cost, or its suitability when interlocked with other events in the programme, or simply by the decision of the production team under the leadership of the editor that another event would be more interesting or more in keeping with the style and reputation of the programme.

Programme-makers also study the breakdown of weekly viewing figures, supplied by an independent market research organisation, to try to assess what the public wants to see, and when. These ratings can be outlined in chart form showing (every fifteen minutes throughout the day) how the pattern of viewing fluctuates between the four channels as viewers switch their allegiance from one to another. These charts can show, for example, the sudden and dramatic sky-rocketing of the BBC's Welsh viewing audience the moment David Coleman hands over to Bill McLaren for live coverage of Wales v England from the cathedral of rugby union football, Cardiff Arms Park. *Grandstand* and *World of Sport* have these charts available, and by studying them over long periods clear patterns can be seen in the viewing habits of the British public. It is then up to the programme-makers as to how they interpret these results and how they will utilise them in the planning of future productions.

There is a certain similarity between the format of both these excellent Saturday sports offerings. First, there is the introduction with the 'tease', a tantalising look at what is in store. Then, since football is our national game, both sides show their review and preview of the soccer scene, *Football Focus* and *On the Ball*, quite early in the programme, before the supporters leave for the matches. Horse racing figures prominently on both channels, with up-to-the-second betting odds and results. Each programme then offers its chosen sports until the half-time football results start arriving. These results are then given, interspersed with half-time reports from selected grounds, followed by more sporting events until the programmes end with the frenzy of presenting the classified football results, racing results and starting prices, news, views, highlights, trailers.

In the vast complex of BBCs Television Centre at White City, London, *Grandstand* is produced from the studio known as TC2. In common with the *World of Sport* studio at London Weekend Television's South Bank premises, the set for each programme remains in place permanently, never being removed to allow other programmes and then rebuilt in time for the following Saturday's effort. There are very good reasons for this. The sets are often in use during the week to record links and items for the Saturday programme. Considerable time and expertise has been devoted to the installation of the complicated communication systems which are vital to these programmes, and it would be precarious, if not downright impossible, to attempt to break these down and then re-assemble them week after week without introducing gremlins into the system. The amount of information which pours into the studios of *Grandstand* and *World of Sport* is vast. There is a non-stop supply of news items, racing results, changes of betting odds and football scores as they happen. A vast army of people on the studio floor are engaged in the continuous task of bringing scoreboards up to date, assembling betting information, editing and rewriting items of news, typing, retyping.

The most important factor in the slick presentation of these types of programmes is the one word 'communications'. Without instant and reliable contact with all the sources needed for the programme the effort of dozens and dozens of people will come to nothing. It is all very well for an OB to be standing by with an interview with the man who has just beaten the world snooker champion, but unless they can inform the studio control room of this, and make provision for the pictures and sound to be transmitted or recorded, they can make no contribution to the programme.

It is irritating for the viewer, too, to be told that he is now going to join the start of the British Grand Prix only to find that he is looking at some coloured vertical bars and listening to a continuous, monotonous note.

Each week, as the OBs move to new sporting venues, engineers pick up the sound and pictures from these locations and 'patch' them to monitors in the control rooms, to the video tape areas, and to the buttons on the vision mixing panels, so that they can be fed into the programmes and thence to the viewer. They also install what is known as DIRT (Directors' Instant Reverse Talkback), which is a technical way of describing the device which enables the studio director to talk to directors and commentators at all outside locations, and them to him. DIRT is vital on these types of programmes.

Grandstand's and *World of Sport*'s control rooms have more than sixty monitors between them to allow for the variety of sources the programme might need in the course of the afternoon's presentation. As an event ends the monitor carrying that OB can be reswitched to carry the pictures from another event yet to happen. Not all the monitors are devoted to the sources the programmes need, however. One monitor shows the output of the rival channel, so that one can see what the other is doing and see, for example, who is winning in the race to be first to provide the final football scores.

Apart from the people on the studio floor and on the OBs, many others are working just as diligently in the video tape areas, recording items and events as they happen, editing them for future use, and playing them into the programme when instructed to do so. As many as half-a-dozen machines at once are engaged in this way, with representatives of the production team timing each event and feeding this information to the control room constantly.

The atmosphere in the control rooms of both *Grandstand* and *World of Sport* is very similar, even if the layout and vocabulary is a little different. There is the same aura of confidence and tension; the same crisp directives and responses; the same professional ability of those in the front line to devote themselves totally to six different matters at once, yet isolating the priority of any particular moment.

On *Grandstand*, the editor sits alongside the director, in constant contact with him and with the anchor man. On *World of Sport*, the editor and his team operate from a room, constructed in the studio itself, just out of shot of the cameras (called the 'fishbowl'). The editor is in contact with the director (in this case a woman), via microphone and speaker and vice versa. The *Grandstand* director can descend a flight of stairs to the studio floor for discussions with the personnel there. If the *World of Sport* director wants to go into the studio she must walk twenty paces to a lift, ascend to the floor above, walk about a hundred paces to another lift which takes her to the door of the studio. Not surprisingly she does not usually leave her control room, and although the presenter can hear the director constantly through his deaf-aid receiver, most of the time it is the editor and his assistants who have the closest personal contact with him.

Both systems have their merits and demerits. The control room of *Grandstand* tends to be a little noisier since the producer is often talking to people on location or in other parts of the building while the director is engaged in issuing instructions into his microphone only inches away from the editor. On *World of Sport* the director is the only person speaking in the control room, although everything she says can be heard by the team in the fishbowl. Any discussions between the editor and OBs or anyone else do not intrude into the control room, and the director converses with the editor only when either of them wishes to.

On *Grandstand*, then, the director has a little more distraction to contend with, but he is constantly aware of all decisions the editor is making. On *World of Sport*, although the director reigns supreme in the control room, she is not involved in the editor's decision-making until her contribution is required. Both systems work admirably, however, and it is unlikely that either programme would wish to change a style of operation that has served them well over the years.

Perhaps the biggest difference between the two programmes lies in the style, personality and delivery of their two main anchor men. David Coleman, for *Grandstand*, and Dickie Davies for *World of Sport* are highly experienced, very professional, and extremely knowledgeable on sporting matters. They are both subjected to tremendous pressures during the course of the afternoon, for the shape of the programme is constantly changing. Sporting events never seem to run to plan on these programmes: a horse race is delayed because of one fractious horse; football matches do not all end conveniently at the same time because of injuries and other factors; a table tennis match takes longer than expected; a vital interviewee cannot be found when needed; a bad crash stops a motor race on the first lap and the restart is held up for fifteen minutes. So it is 'In the meantime let's go back to the studio....' Back in the studio it is the anchor man who has to chat to the viewer while new instructions are shouted into his earpiece: 'Forget about the swimming, Dickie, it's too long. Link us into the boxing ... fast!' or 'David, three items of news and then we'll go to Arsenal for a half-time report by John ... stand by, Arsenal ... what do you mean you're not ready? Forget it David, link to Wolves.'

That sort of one-way conversation is the lot of the anchor man for much of the afternoon's transmission, and even experienced programme-makers still wonder at the ability of men like Coleman and Davies to maintain their calm whilst being subjected to non-stop chatter and constant changes of direction.

When Coleman walks into the studio he brings with him tremendous presence, drive, and authority. It is impossible not to know that he is there! He has a personal charm which switches itself off instantly if he comes up against incompetence or those who cannot keep pace with his thoughts. While writing a link into an item he demands that a monitor be fitted immediately into the space on his desk, then chats in a charming manner to the director about a mutual friend. Four technicians arrive in seconds and the monitor is installed.

He offers suggestions ceaselessly, and is not content to accept any shot the director takes of him if he is not happy with it. He checks the pictures on the bank of monitors behind him, and speaks his mind if he finds any fault. Those on top of their job can find working with him stimulating, if exhausting. He does not suffer fools gladly, and woe betide the bungler, the inexpert.

His mind never stops racing, and his machine-gun delivery sometimes leaves his tongue trying to keep pace with his brain. His sporting knowledge is legendary, however, and his ability to recall facts uncanny. During a lull in the programme Coleman checks his facts with a football sub-editor: 'Crystal Palace haven't lost at home for how many games? Six ... OK. When was the last time Everton lost away to Liverpool? If Aberdeen lose and Celtic win how will that affect the top of the table?' The information goes into his computer-like brain. Nearly two hours later, as the results tumble in on the video-printer, he recalls these facts, never once glancing at his notes. 'Leeds 1, Chelsea 2. That is the first win for Chelsea since early October.'

Dickie Davies has this ability, too. In both their cases this knowledge of facts is not confined to football. Certainly they are both primed by experts and reams of paper information, but recalling these facts with less than a second's hesitation while a director and editor scream into their earpieces on another matter is a measure of how much they are both on top of their craft.

Dickie Davies brings a gentler approach to his job. He is universally loved, both within and outside the profession. He is no less demanding, no less intolerant of incompetence, no slower on his feet; but his

Welsh charm creates less tension. He laughs readily, but can be tough when needed.

These two presenters spearhead the output of the programmes, an output that involves the efforts of so many other people. Of course, Saturday afternoon is simply the climax of a week or more of preparation. Films have to be shot; sporting events recorded and edited; commentaries written and dubbed onto items. Once again scripts, information, facts and figures all consume reams and reams of paper.

Most events are planned months in advance. In the case of *World of Sport* they rely on the OB units from other ITV companies to cover the events happening in their particular area: Granada OBs cover matches at Liverpool; HTV the golf from Chepstow. So there is much forward planning with other companies when their resources are needed.

The production teams from both programmes are particularly experienced in linking up with items being televised on the Continent, or even further afield. They both have good contacts with all major foreign television companies and there is a ready interchange of televised sporting events.

Sometimes they send their own commentators to major foreign events like top athletics meetings. Here the scene is remarkable. As many as twenty different television companies from more than a dozen countries might want facilities to video tape the event, recording their own commentator's voice over the general sounds from the stadium. These requests are made and implemented months ahead, so on arrival the commentators are shown to their position and provided with headphones, microphones and monitors. Video tape machines are allocated to each company represented, recording the pictures and sound from the ground plus the particular commentator's voice.

British commentators sit between their excitable Italian and Greek counterparts. From the twenty or so commentary positions it seems that all Europe is represented and speaking at once, but it all works in the end. The host company also provides facilities for individual commentators to deliver pieces to camera (both live and recorded) and for interviews to be conducted. This all needs planning and careful scheduling, hence the need for forward thinking by everyone.

Sometimes, as in the case of the FA Cup Final, both *Grandstand* and *World of Sport* revolve around this one event, and there is healthy competition between them to tempt the viewer to switch to their particular channel. Both programmes seek out the most famous, exciting and informed guests to bolster their coverage of the game. Both search for novelty in the build-up to the match; both have their panel of experts who will analyse and expound before, during and after the final.

Between them, the BBC and ITV place more than two dozen cameras at Wembley to televise the game from all angles, to service their studios at the ground, to pick up the atmosphere both inside and outside the stadium, in the players' tunnel and the dressing rooms, and to cover the presentation of the cup and medals at the Royal Box. It is a prodigious effort for that one event alone, but the viewer still gets his share of horse racing (television's most covered sport) and other events until the start of the main cup final build-up.

Saturday follows Saturday relentlessly, and for those engaged on these programmes there is no respite from the never-ending need to supply the viewer with the best sporting action they can muster each week. Ironically, all those working on *Grandstand* and *World of Sport* have little opportunity to watch sport during the programme as a viewer would. After cutting to a live or recorded sporting event the production team concentrate on what they will do when the item comes to an end. Highlights of last Thursday's boxing at the Albert Hall, or live rally-cross, cannot be enjoyed by those in the control room. They are simply blocks of action lasting so many minutes: minutes when decisions can be made.

The editor speaks to the director and the presenter together. 'We'll come out of this to three bits of news, then link us to a half-time report from Spurs if they're ready, if not we'll go to Liverpool.' The PA cuts in. 'Three minutes left on this item.' The director leans towards the microphone. 'Spurs! We'll be coming to you in about two-and-a-half minutes. Will you be ready?'

'Hard to say. We've had a lot of injuries.'

'Liverpool! We might come to you before Spurs.'

'Understood.'

'How long on this item?'

'Two minutes twenty.'

'Spurs have gone three up!'

Down in the studio an operator types out the score on a special machine which offers this score on one of the monitors.

'OK! Stand by to super this. Super it. Lose it.'

'One minute forty-five seconds on this item.'

'Any slides needed for these news items?'

'Yes! Keegan, Barry Sheene and Steve Davis. They're standing by.'

'Good! How long to go?'

'One minute.'

'It's half-time at Liverpool.'

'Great! Liverpool we'll be coming to you first now in about one minute forty.'

'You've got to be joking!'

'I'm not. Stand by.'

'Coming off this item in ten, nine, eight... '

'Stand by, studio! Cue and take. Coming to slide next. Stand by, Liverpool ... about twenty seconds. Take slide. Lose it.'

'It's half-time at Spurs.'

'We'll take them after Liverpool. Slide next. Take it. Lose it. Stand by, Liverpool. Coming to you Spurs in about a minute. We want forty-five seconds from you, Liverpool.'
'We'll be ready in thirty seconds.'
'Can't you make it sooner? Give us another news story. Give us the nod as soon as you're ready, Liverpool. Take slide. Lose it.
'They're ready at Anfield.'
'Good! Link to Liverpool. Coming to you Anfield. Take Liverpool.'
'Forty seconds left on this.'
'Coming back to studio then to Spurs. Are you ready, Spurs?'
'Just getting the camera round to John.'
'Well, hurry it up.'
'Ten seconds on this.'
'Wind it up Liverpool. Coming to studio. Cue and take. Stand by, Spurs!'
'Standing by.'
'Take Spurs. Well done everyone.'
'Forty seconds on this.'
'How are the half-time scores doing?'
'We've got most of them.'
'Good. We'll go to them next. Stand by studio with half-time scores.'
'Spurs have finished.'
'Blast! Take studio. What were Spurs playing at? Take half-time scores.'
'Out of this to racing results. How many are there?'
'Seven, ending on the three-thirty from Doncaster.'
'Fine! What's the state of the rally-cross?'
'They're holding the start of the next race. How long will it be before we take them?'
'What do you think? Two minutes? With you in about two minutes rally-cross. Stand by with racing results.'

That control room chatter is typical of what the presenter hears through his earpiece during the programme, which he must listen to and act upon without allowing it to distract him from what he is saying to the viewer at the time. It is typical of the fluctuating nature of the programme and the constant need for alertness and quick decision-making by the production team.

There are rare moments when they can relax, and their period of greatest and most unpredictable activity occurs when they are most battle-weary – towards the end of the programme. This is when the final football scores pour in and are entered on special boards in the studio. Racing results, too, are brought up to date; major news items edited and written; graphics showing the top and bottom of the league tables assembled. There are full time reports from soccer OBs to be cut to. Recorded highlights on video tape are stood ready to be fed into the programme.

Then, suddenly, it is almost over.
'That's it for this week. Don't forget live soccer on Wednesday, seven-thirty. Next Saturday, live athletics from Crystal Palace. See you then. Good afternoon.'
'Cue music. Roll roller.'
'Forty-five seconds to off air . . . five, four, three, two, one . . . that's it, we're off!'
'Well done, everyone. Nicely done, Jean. Thanks, Gerry.'
The familiar release of tension and mild euphoria is everywhere. Thanks are meted out over-enthusiastically, mistakes forgiven, rapports re-established.

Those who give up their Saturdays each week to walk the tightrope of producing programmes like *Grandstand* and *World of Sport* (not forgetting those who work on breakfast television and Saturday morning shows) are among the most competent professionals in the television industry. They have to be. Five hours or so of operating on the knife-edge of nervous energy is not for everyone. For those who make it their lives there is no substitute for the excitement, the adrenalin-pumping stimulation that comes from involvement in these programmes. They tend to work hard and play hard. They are the élite of live television.

12 DOCUMENTARIES

We looked at location filming earlier when considering the role of news camera teams. These work as small, compact, relatively inconspicuous bodies which are highly mobile and versatile. Cameramen usually shoot either with video cameras using video tape, or with film cameras using what we call reversal film. This type of film, after being processed, produces a single positive print, which can then be quickly cut up and edited into a story for the next available news bulletin or magazine programme. That item is usually the one and only moment of glory for reversal film. The unused shots (called trims) are later destroyed, and the news item itself stored in the film library, perhaps to re-emerge years later if the story makes the news once more.

Documentary filming, however, where the quality of the film in the finished product is more important than speed, is normally shot on quite different film stock. This is referred to as negative (or sometimes neg/pos) film which, after processing, produces a master negative of everything which has been filmed, and from which any number of positive prints can be run off.

This valuable negative is stored in a safe place until needed later, while a positive copy arrives in the hands of the man who will physically edit the material into the finished documentary – the film editor. These first reels of film run off from the negative are called the 'rushes', since they are rushed through the printing stage to the editor with not too much concern for optimum picture quality. We shall study what happens to these rushes later.

Firstly, however, before the film can be shot there must be a subject about which someone wishes to make a documentary film (we touched on this in the chapter investigating how television programmes come into being). It might seem a ridiculously obvious statement to make if we say that the style of the finished documentary depends very much on the style of the men who will spearhead the making of it. Let us just consider this, however.

Ask twenty people to visit a museum and later write down their impressions and there are likely to emerge twenty, quite different, versions of the value or otherwise of the place. In the same way, since documentaries are programmes which reflect someone's view of an aspect of life on this planet, the choice of that 'someone' is crucial to the shape of the final product. Quite often this 'someone' is made up of three different professional programme-makers: the producer, director and reporter.

The producer's main responsibility is to control the overall shape of the film, the balance between the fors and againsts of the treatment of the subject, the direction which the programme takes, the choice of who should and who should not appear, the final arbiter and keeper of the purse. The director's function, as ever, is to direct the film unit in such a way as to capture the essence of the subject in the agreed style, and inevitably to add his personal touch to the treatment. The reporter, of course, is the 'front of camera' man who conducts all interviews, who talks to the viewer through the lens of the camera ('pieces to camera' as they are called), and who will write and deliver unseen the important commentary in the finished programme.

In an ideal world all three should work in total harmony, all agreeing on the form the film is to take, with the way it is shaping during shooting, and on the treatment of the subject during the editing, leading to the end product – the documentary programme. That is in an ideal world. In practice it does not always work out quite like this, because all three are usually creative men in their own right, with firm, personal views on any subject and their specialised, individual, artistic means of expressing these views on film. It is for these qualities that they were employed in the first place, for no television company can succeed with grey, acquiescent programme-makers in the van of their productions.

The programme, then, is likely to emerge as a product of the inevitable clashes between all three, with each succeeding and conceding during the making of the film. This is not necessarily a bad thing. It might need the reporter to remind the director that he is being carried away by his filming and losing the thread of the subject. It is no bad lesson for the reporter to be reminded by the producer that the documentary is supposed to be looking at a certain subject and that it is not a vehicle for said reporter to parade in front of his public whilst wooing them with poignant prose and scintillating syntax.

The best documentaries, then, are often the result of this chemical process involving the talents and personalities of these three human elements. As ever, there are exceptions to this tried and trusted method of programme-making. Sometimes the three elements are combined in one man, who is producer, director and reporter. He decides on the shape of the programme, and on the style of shooting the editing. He carries out all interviews on film, writes and speaks the commentary; in fact he does everything, with no-one to restrain him or criticise his efforts.

This method of documentary-making is full of dangers. The load on one man, satisfying though it might be, is very heavy. There is the obvious risk of complacency, of the programme becoming too biased in a certain direction without, perhaps, the maker being aware of this.

There is the risk of self-indulgence in the choice of interviewees or in the selection of their answers from the dozens or hundreds which will be discarded.

To avoid these pitfalls and still emerge with a balanced, interesting programme which is 'good television' requires a special kind of talent. Such men do exist. We mentioned earlier the award-winning producer/director/reporter, John Willis, whose first major work *Johnny Go Home* shocked the country into realising the plight of homeless young boys in London. He followed this with many more in the vein of investigative journalism, always probing, never afraid to pursue the subject if he felt that there was something unpleasant or illegal or socially disgraceful which should be made public in the interests of a civilised society. His *Rampton – The Secret Hospital* opened viewers' (and authority's) eyes to the conditions in Britain's criminal asylums, leading to charges being brought against individuals, and changes being demanded at government level.

There are others with this brand of talent, but they are a rare breed. So it is usually a team effort which leads to the successful documentary, and in some cases this can involve as many as a dozen people engaged on location shooting anywhere in the world. Moving this unit around with their dozen or so boxes of equipment can be an expensive and troublesome operation.

Since documentaries concern themselves with capturing an aspect of life as it happens, there is a limit to how much can be preplanned when considering the shooting of the programme over a period of many weeks. The people appearing in the film are not actors contracted for the programme and paid to do the director's bidding. Scenes cannot be carefully set up and rehearsed, and there is rarely the added luxury of re-shooting them if they do not come up to expectations. Documentary-makers tend to work fast on location, and must be prepared to change their plans if the story they are telling changes direction or takes on an added twist which cannot be ignored.

Imagine, for example, that the closing credits are rolling through the screens at the end of a sporting documentary showing two weeks in the life of Kelly, a soccer superstar; two weeks in which his team played two Saturday league games plus a mid-week semi-final match in a European Cup Competition in Paris. It has been an absorbing insight into the player's world, with much exciting action and personal revelations. Let us look at how the documentary was made.

Of course the player himself must agree to the film being made in the first place or there would be no point in going any further with the project. Then his manager must be approached, for without his co-operation, too, the film is doomed.

These two vital participants may be contacted in a variety of ways. Sometimes it is best if the producer makes the early approaches, or maybe a researcher. Often, though, the programme-makers employ the services of a go-between, a reporter, a friend of the family, or a playing colleague to broach the subject in the first place, and later to introduce the two factions to each other on an amicable basis.

Eventually, Kelly and the manager agreed to talk to the production team and a meeting took place. The participants for their part wished to know the form the programme would take, who would be the reporter, how much the film unit would intrude into their lives, where they wished to film and when, who else they wished to interview and so on. The fees each would receive were discussed and agreed. The production team were looking for total co-operation from the player and manager, and that included invasion of domestic privacy, disruption of home life, the involvement of wives and children, and, above all, total honesty from everyone in the telling of the story. Co-operation was promised.

In addition, both parties went into details of actual filming dates, times and locations. For example, the director wanted permission to take his film crew into the team's dressing room before and after a game, and at half-time. These are tense moments for professional sportsmen so the player's team mates needed to be consulted and reassurances given that the film crew would be discreet and as unassuming as possible. The director agreed to keep the number of crew members on those occasions to a minimum.

Then there was the important matter of shooting the player in action. Camera positions were agreed, and facilities given to allow the unit to move freely around the ground in their search for close, intimate action. The director wished to place a microphone on the manager during the course of a match in the hope that some choice, and transmittable, comments would give added reality to the programme. This was agreed.

Kelly's wife, vital to the success of the film for she can reveal much about the man behind the star, was taken to dinner with her husband and the early indications were that she was keen to help but a little shy. During the filming she would be encouraged to speak frankly about the man in her life. What kind of husband is he? Is he a good father? Does he get nervous on the day of a match? How does he relax? What are his hobbies, and what kind of holidays does he like to take? The co-operation of the wife on questions like these can give an insight into the player which is unique and privileged.

She could well also be of interest in her own right. Does she get nervous when he is to play? Does she watch him in action or not? How does she react to the adulation he receives wherever they go, and the constant demands on their time by the media, and the intrusion of autograph hunters, well-wishers, critics and camp-followers? What effect does his stardom have on the lives of his children at school and play? Does she want her sons to be footballers? How has she adjusted to the high standard of living and the luxury life his talents have given her? Does she worry about injury, the days when he can no longer play, or possible loss of form with the attendant decrease in his value as a player?

These and dozens more questions would be put to her by the reporter during the making of the film, so it was essential that she respected and trusted him or the real truth would not emerge. The reporter must command the same respect from the manager, other players, the club's directors and anyone else he wished to interview. These pre-filming meetings, winings and dinings were pleasant but necessary preliminaries to the actual shooting.

The production team (the producer, director, PA, reporter and researcher) planned the two weeks of filming.

Monday: General shots of Kelly training.

Tuesday, Wednesday and Thursday: Exteriors and interiors around his house, including him playing with children, relaxing indoors. Also sequences to be filmed of him at his favourite relaxation – angling. Main interview with wife.

Friday: Main interview with his manager. Also chats to three of his team mates. In evening, film him at a social evening with supporters club, signing autographs and generally mingling. Impromptu chats with selected supporters.

Saturday: Travel with Kelly to football ground. Shots in dressing room before game, at half-time and at end. Shots of him playing in between. Brief interview with him afterwards.

Sunday: Pack film equipment and prepare to travel to Paris.

Monday: Morning – flight to Paris, check equipment through customs. Afternoon – film Kelly and his team arriving at Paris airport, travel and film with team on coach to hotel. Check into hotel.

Tuesday: Film him training and sight-seeing around Paris.

Wednesday: Travel with him to match. Film him in action, followed by interview with him at end of game.

Thursday: Pack equipment and return to England.

Friday: Pick-up day, i.e. any shots, sequences or interviews still outstanding.

Saturday: Final shots of him in action at league match. Final interview with him.

The PA moved into action. She typed out the shooting shedule and sent copies, dozens of them, to everyone who needed them – the film crew of course, various departmental heads, the film manager's office, the film editor, and even the company doctor who must be informed if anyone is injured or taken ill on location.

The PA then organised air tickets for the flight to Paris and back, and booked each member of the film team into a Paris hotel for three nights, not forgetting to arrange for a room to be hired at the hotel where the film equipment could be stored each night. Then there were cars and station wagons to be hired in Paris to accommodate the crew plus all their equipment, with a separate car for the production team who might sometimes have appointments independently from the film crew.

She then estimated how much money she would need (both in sterling and in French francs) and collected this from the accounts department. She checked that each member of the crew had a valid passport, and organised money for them if required.

Taking very expensive, professional film equipment into a foreign country is regarded seriously by customs officials. Forms must be completed well in advance detailing every single piece of equipment carried, including serial numbers and all means of identification. When leaving the country the customs officials will want to be satisfied that what went into the country leaves the country – nothing more and nothing less. The film section is well versed in these requirements and the forms were prepared in good time.

The director and cameraman discussed how much film stock they might need, especially for the trip to France, and this was ordered. The film stock usually comes in cans containing 400 feet of film (allowing roughly $10\frac{1}{2}$ minutes of shooting time). They are normally packed in boxes holding nine cans, and constitute a bulky and heavy item.

In the meantime the researcher had been busy. She had already made one trip to Paris to smooth arrangements for the crew to film at the important match, arranging press passes and car parking space at the ground. She had also visited the supporters club in England and ensured a good turn out for the filming on the first Friday. She knew she would probably see little of the actual filming for she would spend much time one jump ahead of the film crew as she double-checked arrangements for the next day's shoot.

The director and the cameraman conferred. It is important that the cameraman understands how the director wants the documentary to be treated, the kind of shots he is interested in and the kind he is not. The cameraman must know how the director wants to arrange the reporter and interviewee during filmed interviews. Is he interested in telephoto lens shots of the players in action? Has he any plans for slow-motion action shots? If so, special equipment must be hired. Does he want to film in poor light conditions without the intrusion of special lighting? If so, then special fast film stock will be needed.

For much of the time during documentary filming there is little opportunity for the director actually to direct the cameraman in the finer points of the coverage of an event or an incident. Life happens without regard for documentary-makers and as each new happening presents itself it is usually up to the cameraman to react quickly and capture the incident *in the style laid down by the director in their pre-shooting chat.* The cameraman must be clear in his own mind, then, what incidents are of interest to the director and react to those only.

The day arrived for filming to begin: Monday of week one. The unit drove up to the footballer's training ground and unloaded their equipment. There were tripods of various heights, and the camera, of course, usually mounted on a smooth-action pan-and-tilt head, or sometimes 'hand held' by the cameraman for greater freedom especially in covering movement. Most of the filming would be done with a zoom lens, but other specialised lenses were carried to accommodate any wide-angle or telephoto filming.

The cameraman's assistant had already loaded the film stock from three of the original cans into special magazines which are attached to the camera during filming. As each magazine of 400 feet of film is exposed, it is replaced with one containing unexposed film and the camera is again ready for use. The assistant then takes the exposed film out of the used magazine and puts it back into the original can, ready to be sent to the processing laboratories. He then reloads the magazine with unexposed film ready for shooting. These operations are carried out blindly by the assistant since they must be performed in a light-proof bag into which he inserts his hands via elasticated openings. It is remarkable how quickly a good assistant can open a reel of film, wind it onto the mechanism of the magazine, close the magazine and have it ready for filming working entirely by feel. Not surprisingly this mobile 'dark-room' is known in the profession as a groping bag!

The sound recordist had his portable recording machine carried via a shoulder strap. He also had a variety of microphones for different circumstances: radio microphones requiring no cables to the recording machine to allow for free action by the users; more substantial, cabled microphones for controlled situations; and the highly directional 'gun mic' which can pick up selected sounds some distance from the camera from the direction in which the microphone is pointed.

Without getting too technical, the speed at which the camera operates must be precisely related to the speed of the spools rotating on the mobile tape recorder if pictures and sound are to be in perfect synchronisation. Manmade pieces of apparatus cannot be relied upon to function to such exact requirements day after day, year after year. Built into the camera, then, is a small crystal which oscillates at a predetermined, never varying frequency, emitting a pulse which controls the speed of the camera. A crystal with identical characteristics in the tape recorder ensures that sound is recorded in relation to the same pulse governing the camera speed, and thereby guaranteeing pictures and sound which are 'in sync'.

These pictures and sounds must be identified back in the film editing rooms so that the separate reels of film can be linked up with the relevant reels of sound. Each new shot that the cameraman takes is numbered chronologically, therefore, by using that familiar piece of film equipment, the clapper board. Most people now understand its function. It carries the title of the programme, and the names of the director and the cameraman. It has space to carry the description of the film stock used, and of course the number of each shot: shot thirty-two, take one . . . shot thirty-three, take one, and so on.

At the commencement of each new shot the sound recordist sets his machine to record, and the reels of tape start to roll. The cameraman then starts his camera and calls for the shot to be 'marked'. The assisant holds the clapper board in front of the camera with the pivoted arm raised and identifies the shot: shot thirty-four, take one. He then snaps the arm shut and removes the board.

When the separate reels of film and sound tape reach the film editor an assistant synchronises the shot of the clapper board arm snapping shut with the sound it makes. He gradually builds up a large reel containing the shots in the order in which they were taken, with sound and pictures perfectly synchronised. It is a tedious vital task which must be accomplished before the producer and director can view the rushes and plan the shape of the programme.

13 SHOOTING THE DOCUMENTARY

It was time for shot one, take one. The camera was set up close to the practice ground, camera and sound recorder switched on, the shot marked and the documentary was under way. By the end of the morning two magazines had been used up on shots of general training by the team, with many close-ups of Kelly in action, chatting with the coach, joking with his team-mates. The director and cameraman had been on the lookout constantly for any incident which revealed anything of the man the fans never get to see: his dedication to the numbingly boring ritual of getting and keeping fit; his application to the down-to-earth business of sharpening his natural ability for the skills of the game; his relationships with his colleagues, and their reaction to the superstar within their midst; his response to coaching and criticism; his willingness or otherwise to integrate with other players and accept a minor role in a practice game.

A further magazine had been exposed on an unscheduled chat with the chief coach, whose no-nonsense attitude to the game and to Kelly himself proved to be an unexpected bonus. The morning had gone well.

The next three days, too, proved satisfactory. The player and his family adjusted surprisingly quickly to the presence of the camera crew (adept at putting people at ease) and the director knew he had plenty of good material showing Kelly as husband, father and man-about-the-house. His wife, too, after an initial period of nervousness (which meant that the first ten minutes or so of filmed interview might just as well be thrown away), eventually responded to the skilled approaches of the reporter and actually seemed to enjoy revealing the harmless intimacies of life with a man revered by many thousands of fans. This was a key interview in the documentary, and the fact that it had gone well was a great relief to the director.

The interview with the manager was less satisfying. He proved to be cautious in his assessment of Kelly as a player. He was obviously reluctant to risk sounding too lavish in his praise for the player's ability for reasons he did not divulge. His answers were clichéd and studied. 'Kelly has been a great asset to the side and we hope his future will be with this club for many years to come . . . There's no doubt that the lad has great natural ability, and no-one works harder at his game than he does . . . He's very popular with the other players, and he's a good family man . . . If he has a fault it's that he holds onto the ball a little too long sometimes: but the lad scores goals and you can't take that away from him.'

During a break while the camera assistant reloaded some magazines the director, producer and reporter conferred. This interview was proving too bland. While not actually seeking sensational revelations for their own sake, they were hoping that the manager would reveal another side to the man, to observe Kelly as a player, warts and all. Kelly's strengths and weaknesses as a player and a man are inseparable from the performance of the side during a match, for his natural genius for the game was the corner stone around which the style of play of the team had been built.

The manager has had to encourage and help develop further this natural ability, without allowing the player to assume that the team could not exist without him. He has had to make him feel important without arousing the resentment of the rest of the other players. He has had to allow Kelly's genius to flower on the field even if this defied a pre-arranged plan, yet he has disciplined, fined and criticised him when needed with no hint of favouritism. He has nurtured him through injuries and given him confidence to throw himself back into the first game following a cartilage operation. On a man to man, boss to employee, mentor to pupil, basis the manager had a unique opportunity to reveal the side of Kelly which the documentary needed and which the viewer would find absorbing. Yet the answers gave nothing away.

The reporter tried again. Another two magazines were wasted while the manager, pleasant but cautious, was incapable of breaking away from the style of replying to news reporters who week after week asked the same questions and seemed satisfied with the same answers. The production team felt they were getting nowhere. The manager could not relax enough with them to break from his method of dealing with questioners – rather like the style adopted by shop stewards who seem to have all read the same training manual on 'dealing with the press'.

There was no point in pursuing the interview further at this stage. Perhaps later in the film shoot there might be an opportunity to catch the manager in a more relaxed, expansive mood. Perhaps as the next few days unfolded he might feel safer, more trustworthy of their presence. For now, however, the interview was over.

The chats with some of Kelly's colleagues proved just as unsatisfactory. Footballers are reluctant to be quoted on their honest opinion of other players, and the replies were again cautious and in some cases frivolous. The evening at the supporters club proved less than successful, also. Too many fans had poured in in an attempt to be seen in front of the camera. There was so much drunken behaviour and childish tomfoolery while interviews were being filmed that the exercise was eventually abandoned, and the crew joined the revellers at the bar. There was little to salvage from the evening's shoot, and the production crew found themselves in the middle-of-filming depression which seems to afflict all documentary-makers at some stage of the shoot.

Tomorrow, however, Kelly would turn out for his club. Until now there had been much film shot on 'talking heads' and soft action. Tomorrow would be when the star moved into the spotlight, on the stage, in his favourite role. Tomorrow he could show the world why he was so adulated, why, in fact, he had been chosen as the subject for the documentary in the first place.

Saturday morning started unhappily for the television team. A report from the film editor who had viewed the rushes of the first few day's shooting stated that, due to a fault during the processing of the film, over half the interview with Kelly's wife was unusable. The sound, of course, was unaffected, so perhaps some of the words she had spoken could be run behind shots relevant to what she had said.

The producer and reporter decided to spend the morning in the film cutting room, studying the extent of the damage to the film. At the same time they planned to listen to the sound of the interview, select those answers most likely to appear in the finished programme, and let the director know if there were sufficient shots to lay behind these spoken words. If there were not, time would have to be found during the coming week to shoot whatever was necessary, for the interview with the wife was a vital ingredient in the documentary.

In addition, the report stated that amongst the film ruined in processing was a never-to-be-recaptured moment during an angling trip when Kelly's only catch of the day fell off the hook at the last second, to the uncontrollable delight of his two children. Lost, too, was a scene where Kelly met his children from school (filmed from a hidden camera) which was charming in its uninhabited spontaneity. This might be possible to film again, time permitting, but there was no guarantee that the magic of the first encounter could be recalled.

Filming Kelly travelling to the ground in his BMW was straightforward, despite the fact that he became a little irritable at having to retrace part of the journey to enable shots to be taken from inside the car. At the ground, pre-match nerves began to take over and he became annoyed when a microphone proved faulty during a 'take' and he refused to co-operate on a second take of the ruined action.

Although the director had taken the precaution of having the electrician install lights in the empty dressing room during the morning, attempts to film the pre-match scenes in there did not work out as planned. Despite an agreement with the manager and players that their presence would be welcome, the crew came in for so much obstruction and abuse from the players that it became obvious that their presence there was not only bad for the footballers, but also was contributing little of value to the documentary. In addition, the good relations built up over the week with Kelly, the manager, and the other players was rapidly turning to unconcealed animosity.

The manager ordered the crew out of the room and a distasteful row broke out between him and the director. The crew snatched a few last shots, but in the end the lights were switched off and the crew moved outside to set up the camera to film the match. The manager made it clear to the now furious director that any attempt to come into the dressing room at half-time would not only lead to them being thrown out but it could well bring any further shooting of the documentary to an end.

The director knew he was beaten. The tension among professional sportsmen before they run out into the cauldron of competition just cannot be compared with the pre-match frolics of Sunday morning village-green games. For the professional, of course, a football match is more than a game. It is the time when he must justify his salary, when he must demonstrate his talents under the microscopic gaze of fans, critics, commentators, managers and other players. It is when he must prove his worth and justify his inclusion in the team and secure his future.

A football pitch is like a gladiatorial arena to him; a place where he will compete with others equally determined to win, to show their worth, their superiority. There is the risk of injury, the fear of personal failure, the possibility of defeat. Outsiders are not welcome in the intimacy and tension of the professionals' dressing room prior to a match.

As the game got under way the cameraman concentrated on Kelly, filming him each time it seemed that the player might become involved in the action. He also took some wide shots of general play to capture the feel of the occasion, and to act as transition shots between one shot of Kelly and another in the editing stage.

Some of the action was very good. Kelly became involved in a number of attacking movements, and only a desperate save by the opposing goalkeeper prevented him scoring. Eventually a well-directed pass from Kelly split the defence and a team-mate drove the ball past the 'keeper for the first goal. The predictable hugs and jubilation followed.

Half-way through the second half Kelly's fortunes, and the shape of the documentary, took a new turn. A brutal tackle from behind brought him down heavily and left him writhing in agony. The referee's whistle brought the game to halt and the trainer racing onto the field.

One glance from the director and the cameraman quickly unscrewed his camera from the tripod and, shooting as he went, he ran onto the field capturing the dramatic moments as the trainer worked on the leg of the agonised Kelly. It was half a minute before the referee realised what was going on and ordered the crew off the field, but by then the shots were in the can.

As the camera whirred from the touchline, the trainer and his assistant half carried Kelly off the pitch to the dug-out where they continued to work on the injured leg. The camera crew moved in, picking up the anxious voices of the trainer and manager, the pictures of their strained faces telling as much as the words.

The injury was bad enough to put Kelly out for the rest of the game. With help he walked slowly towards the dressing room with the resilient camera crew at his heels. At the dressing room door angry officials turned them away, but the director knew that a telling sequence has been captured. He had no wish for Kelly to be injured, but it is an occupational hazard among professional players and therefore he regarded it as relevant to the documentary to film such an incident should it happen.

After the game the manager allowed them a short interview in the dressing room with a subdued Kelly occasionally interjecting.

'Yes, it was a badly strained thigh muscle but without major complications.'

'No, it was not a fair tackle and the referee should have sent the defender off the field.'

'Well the physiotherapist has seen him and he'll let us know just how bad it is soon.'

'It's hard to say if he'll miss the Paris match. My guess is that we'll keep him back here for treatment until Tuesday morning, then if he looks okay he'll fly over later that morning to join the rest of the team for some light training and a final checkout on Wednesday morning. We need him in Paris . . . he'll play if it's at all possible.'

The director called the team together. New plans had to be made. Sunday, scheduled as a day for packing the equipment and getting it to the airport, would now have to be devoted to Kelly's medical treatment, an interview with the physiotherapist, and perhaps a short filmed chat with his anxious wife. Monday morning, too, had to be rescheduled for filming the progress of treatment, with the afternoon given over to preparing the equipment for the trip to Paris. The director decided that the crew should travel on the same flight as Kelly, if possible, with the possibility of 'in air' shots as a bonus.

The PA sighed and reached for a telephone. There were air tickets to cancel and new ones to be ordered. The hotel booking in Paris had to be changed and the hire car arrangements altered. Once the flight was confirmed the researcher was despatched to the airline for permission to film aboard the aircraft. This meant an alteration in the customs declarations, for part of the film equipment would be needed in flight and the rest would travel 'freight' as originally intended. That would probably lead to confusion and trouble at Paris but it could not be helped.

Sunday and the morning of Monday went well for the television team. Kelly's injury responded to treatment and he gradually became his jovial self again. The interview with his wife, which concentrated on her reaction to her husband's injury and fears for the future, was worthwhile, and also made up for some of the lost interview. The physiotherapist, however, proved to be rather uncommunicative and predictable.

The crew packed the film equipment on the Monday afternoon, getting it onto a late evening flight to Paris ready for collection the next day. They kept back only the equipment and film stock needed for the journey, together with the appropriate documents. The filming during the flight went well, with a confident Kelly responding lucidly to the reporter's questions. The director looked forward to a sequence in Paris as Kelly travelled to the hotel, met up with his team-mates, and conversed with his manager. It was not to be. There was trouble at the customs shed. Confusion over the alteration of the original documents, the splitting up of the equipment, and the in-flight arrangements which they knew nothing about led to heated exchanges, many telephone calls and further form-filling.

Kelly's taxi whisked him away while the crew battled with bureaucracy. It was nearly midnight before all the equipment was finally released, and all hope of the filmed arrival sequence was lost. Only good thinking by the PA, who made a telephone call to the Paris hotel, ensured (just in time) that their rooms were not allocated to others. In the event, the hotel restaurant had closed by the time the crew arrived, and they settled for sandwiches and coffee.

The following morning, Wednesday, the day of the match, Kelly had a work-out with the team and his injured leg given a thorough testing. It stood up well, although still painful, and it was decided that he would play, with strapping and a pain-killing injection. Kelly co-operated in filming a sight-seeing sequence, and with some general views of Paris to round off the afternoon the director was satisfied.

After the excitement of the past few days things went surprisingly smoothly for the television team at the match. Their passes were in order, their camera position allowed good coverage of the game, the floodlights were excellent, and Kelly's team won by one goal to nil. Kelly himself played a relatively subdued game, although once again he was involved in the move which led to the only goal of the match.

There was much jubilation after the game at the players' hotel, giving a nice film sequence, and the crew's spirits were high again. It was decided to spend the following morning in Paris as a well-earned break and fly back to England with the equipment late afternoon. It was a pleasant morning for everyone except the PA who spent her time on the telephone re-arranging flights and extending hire car bookings.

Friday was spent retaking some of the sequences ruined during film processing, particularly the scene where Kelly met his children from school. As feared, it was not as charismatic as the first attempt, but it was better than nothing.

Saturday's match at last brought the hoped-for goal from Kelly; a movement set in motion by him deep in his own half and rounded off with a diving header. This effort, however, took him out of the match, since he landed awkwardly on his injured leg. Once again the film crew trailed him to the dressing room and while he was being treated the reporter took the opportunity of a final interview before they were all ushered away.

Some days later, as the director and producer viewed the rushes of the two weeks' filming, the form of the programme began to take shape in their minds. Some sequences had turned out better than expected, some more disappointing – as usual. Transcripts were typed, setting out every word spoken on every interview and the two men selected the sections they thought to be most interesting. The related pictures and sound were detached from the rushes and set aside for late editing.

Over the next couple of weeks they both spent long hours in the film cutting room, arguing over which were the most potent sections of interviews, the best shots or the most dramatic sound. The film editor skilfully assembled the selected shots, building up sequences as instructed, but always ready with suggestions for improvement.

As we pointed out in the last chapter, if ten documentary programme-makers were each given a copy of the rushes we would almost certainly end up with ten different documentaries. Each would structure the film along the lines of his own interpretation of the story, and the choice of pictures and sound would be a very personal one.

In the case of the Kelly documentary the producer assumed most of the responsibility for deciding on the shape of the programme, the choice of sections of interviews to be included, and he suggested the action sequences he thought worth including. The director and film editor constructed the film along the lines laid down varying the pace and controlling the dramatic impact by their careful choice of shots and by utilising the skilled techniques of film editing.

Here and there they deviated from the producer's suggestions for one reason or another. Some were accepted, others rejected, sometimes there was compromise. Over the weeks the film took on a positive identity.

The first version of the film assembled from hundreds of shots joined by sticky tape ran sixty-eight minutes or so, more than sixteen minutes too long. The film went back onto the editing machine and sequences were pruned, shots were deleted, action was tightened up, interviews were further edited. Running time was now fifty-three minutes twenty-three seconds, still more than the fifty-two minutes' length required. After more surgery, including the reluctant dropping of what was left of the sequence at the supporters' club, the film ran for the exact scheduled time.

The 'cutting copy' of the film, as it is called at this stage in its life, was despatched to the negative cutting department, where the original negative of every foot of film shot during the fortnight was stored. For days the negative cutters extracted the negative of each shot on the cutting copy, gradually assembling a negative version of the film which was an exact replica, frame by frame, of the film editor's cutting copy. This finally assembled negative version was then sent to the laboratories where a carefully prepared and colour-graded positive print was prepared from the negative. This 'answer print', as it is called, was then sent to the editor where it was scrutinised for any flaws in quality, and notes were made of these imperfections.

Acting on these notes the laboratories ran off a second print which was perfectly satisfactory. This was now the 'transmission copy', the actual film which the viewer would see when the programme would be transmitted.

While the visual side of the documentary was receiving all this attention, the film editor, using his cutting copy which had been returned from the negative cutters, began to assemble the half-a-dozen or so sound tapes which would later be blended into one composite sound track.

This is an important stage in the compilation of a film documentary. The sound which is recorded while the camera films a scene is rarely sufficient on its own to sustain the dramatic value the shot might be capable of. Take the scene where Kelly was first injured. The sound recorded at the time was a little patchy as the sound recordist ran after the cameraman who had chased onto the field to film the player writhing on the grass. As Kelly was treated and led off, the microphone mainly picked up the snatches of conversations between him and the trainer as and when it could be pointed in the right direction.

In the final version of the scene, however, the director wanted a more dramatic treatment of the sound than that. He wanted the reporter to lead the viewer into the impact of the incident. 'And then, suddenly, one tackle changed everything!' Then, as Kelly was scythed to the ground, the director wanted a huge crowd roar, mingled with the long blast of the referee's whistle (not picked up by the microphone at the time). As the referee spoke to the culprit 'crowd booing' was needed, which would overlap onto the further shots of Kelly's treatment on the pitch. As the player was helped to the dressing room the director decided to bring in the voice of the manager (recorded after the game itself) to give more dramatic appeal. 'When I saw him go down I could see it could be a bad one. I must admit my first thoughts were about the match in Paris the following Wednesday ... we knew how badly we needed him. Then I just kept hoping that he hadn't broken it ... for the lad's sake as much as ours. I knew I couldn't concentrate on the match until the doc had seen him. "Don't let it be broken," that's all I could think, "don't let it be broken ...".' The manager's voice tailed away and the roar of the crowd became muted as Kelly neared the dressing room. All these various sound sources, then, were assembled on different reels by the film editor, each foot of sound tape carefully synchronised with the film itself.

It was time for the commentary to be written to fit those parts of the documentary which needed explanations, guidance or dramatic force. Commentary writing is an exercise in the economy of words. The best commentaries gently nudge the documentary along, unobtrusively taking the viewer by the hand and leading him through the programme. So the reporter worked at his typewriter following the instructions of the producer and director. 'Six seconds leading us into the chat with the manager. Fifteen seconds setting up the arrival at the ground. Eight seconds explaining the throwing out of the dressing room. Twenty seconds leading to the injury.'

This commentary was then recorded by the reporter sitting in a sound-proof cubicle, and the reel containing the result added to the other reels containing the voices, sound effects, music and so on which would make up the final sound track.

Without being too technical, the man who produces this sound track, the dubbing mixer, is a highly skilled operator who can do wonders for a film. In his sophisticated dubbing suite the film and the reels of sound are laced onto synchronised rotating spools. As these spools rotate he manipulates the sound from these different reels, recording the result of his efforts onto the tape which will eventually carry the composite sound track of the programme. He often augments these reels of sound with cartridges from his own vast library of sound effects. Over the years dubbing mixers build up this library from the sound tapes which pass through their hands, and from friendly film

Some of the dubbing mixer's store of sound effects tapes.

recordists who bring back unusual sounds from all parts of the globe. Looking at these shelves of sound effects makes interesting and amusing reading: soldiers marching across wooden bridge; non-English shouts; big plane landing; hungry cat eating; African in pain; car refusing to start; referee's whistle (long, short, repeated, urgent, final).

Once the last frame has rolled off the film spool and the last notes of the closing music are recorded, the programme is complete – ready for transmission. Perhaps twenty times more film than it took to compile the transmission copy will never be seen. These trims, as they are called, will eventually be destroyed, except for those shots which someone might find useful for another programme, or which are deemed worth keeping as library film.

Often, a sound track is made excluding the commentary, and called the M and E track, standing as it does for 'music and effects'. This is useful if the programme is sold later to a foreign country, say Japan. Using the M and E track, and with a copy of the commentary script, the commentary can be translated into Japanese and then dubbed onto a composite sound track for the benefit of the viewers in that country.

It is impossible in the space of one chapter to describe fully the thoughts and techniques which go into the making of a documentary. The simple example we looked at was meant to give some idea of the peaks and troughs of this type of programme-making. Life takes its own course, and the documentary-maker must accept that he will have to compromise constantly between what he wants and what he can get. When life does become capricious or downright unfair, he must learn to live with this, adjust his thinking and if possible capitalise on the direction his programme must now follow.

The subject of the documentary is what the programme is about: but it is the documentary-maker who gives it the individual touch which puts it into the award-winning class, or condemns it to mediocrity. Documentary filming, also, is more than a chance to travel the world and shoot exciting or interesting subjects. It is, ultimately, a responsibility which cannot be treated lightly.

Any subject can be slanted either way by a careless, unscrupulous or irresponsible programme-maker. Indeed, in many repressed countries it is one of the methods employed by the State to ensure that the people believe what the government wants them to believe. Even in the free world the dividing line between the enthusiastic manipulation of sound and pictures to make a dramatic point and the actual bending of the truth (accidental or deliberate) can be a very fine one indeed. This applies to much of television, of course; but there is a credibility about the documentary which places it in this unique position of influence. It is a danger of which all those engaged in this type of work must be aware.

14 BEHIND THE SCENES

Visitors to television studios are usually surprised by the large number of people involved in the making of a programme. They expect to see three or four cameramen, perhaps a sound technician or two, and are not surprised by the presence of someone wearing 'cans' who seems to be in charge on the studio floor – in fact the floor manager is often wrongly assumed to be the director.

What does surprise them is the high proportion of apparent hangers-on. Studios in action, of course, are no places for hangers-on, so what visitors are seeing are people who, while they might have no particular function at that moment, have been and will be needed at some time. Stage hands who have brought in and assembled the set will have other duties during the course of a programme, as will props men. Cameramen often need 'trackers' to assist them in moving around the studio floor. The floor manager's assistant, the stage manager, wardrobe staff, carpenters, painters, electricians, autocue operators, make-up girls, extras, interviewees . . . they all need to be there.

We looked at the control rooms earlier with the director, producer, PA, vision mixer, technical supervisor, lighting director, console operator, vision control engineer, sound balancer and tape operator. We know, too, that somewhere else in the building are the telecine and video tape operators. There are transmission controllers and master control engineers, and everyone assumes that there must be more technicians and maintenance men on call when needed. Let us consider, however, those the visitor can only guess at, or which have not or could not occur to him.

There are the usual areas, as in all large organisations, which exist to handle the responsibilities and problems surrounding the employment of a great number of people: personnel, wages, welfare, feeding, health, pensions, safety. There is senior management, of course, where the major decisions are made, and middle management where they are implemented.

There is a vast back-up of office staff behind the making of any television programme. Television simply devours paper, for example, and this calls for many secretaries, copy-takers, script typists, duplicating departments, libraries, contracts departments, accounts sections, and many more. All these people exist for one purpose – to assist in the making of television programmes. However, there are other areas devoted to the selling of programmes after transmission to other companies and to other countries. In commercial television, too, the all-important sales department exists to persuade advertisers to buy time during the commercial breaks, the main source of revenue for independent television companies.

While looking at ITV we must not forget that although there are fifteen self-contained companies supplying television programmes to their allotted areas, there must be some collusion between them when it comes to the transmission of peak-time television. A glance at the menu for an evening's viewing will reveal that from around six-thirty in the evening until ten-thirty at night all companies are usually showing identical programmes. We have already looked at the function of the transmission controllers who have the responsibility of retaining the synchronisation of programmes and commercial breaks throughout a day's transmissions.

In addition, each company has a department, the presentation department, which is responsible for controlling and co-ordinating the presentation of the company's output. As part of its function it provides transmission controllers with a schedule, carefully prepared in advance, to which they must work. This schedule, finalised late afternoon, details the composition of every second that the company will transmit the following day. It lays out in chronological order the exact running time of every programme and a breakdown of how every second of each commercial break is to be filled.

When considering the transmission of peak-time television, it is evident that every presentation department throughout the network must at some time get together to agree and synchronise the second-by-second breakdown of a day's viewing. Every company needs to know the running time of Granada's *Coronation Street*, and of the quiz game from Thames Television which will follow it, for example. The exact location and duration of commercial breaks must be agreed and adhered to.

This getting-together is usually effected twice a day – at mid-morning and late afternoon. At the instigation of the London-based ITV company (Thames or London Weekend) every other company's presentation department is summoned to a conference by telephone. In each department a special 'red phone' buzzes and is answered until all independent television companies are on the line and in mutual contact with each other.

At the morning conference the breakdown of the rest of the day ahead is carefully and chronologically detailed and confirmed. Although the length of commercial breaks are synchronised here, it is the responsibility of each company, of course, to determine how and with what those breaks are to be filled. At this conference, too, any previous arrangement by one or more companies to deviate from the network plan is confirmed. In addition the schedule for the following day is gone through as far as known programme timings will allow.

The late afternoon telephone get-together discusses any last minute changes, and confirms such detail as the names of the ITN newscasters so that local announcers can mention them when linking into these national news bulletins. This meeting is useful, too, for other reasons. Occasionally programmes for transmission that evening have been assembled during that day, and it is not until this multi-phone-in that the company providing that programme can announce its exact running time to the rest of the network.

It is not unknown for those programmes edited on the day of transmission to run shorter or longer than their allocated time, extending or decreasing the length of the commercial breaks around them. Provided the under-run is around ten or twenty seconds most companies can find something to occupy the extension of the break, as we shall see in a moment. When a programme over-runs its scheduled time, however, it can cause headaches throughout the network, particularly among those companies who have packed every second of their expected commercial break with adverts. Programme-makers whose programmes run over time at the last minute are extremely unpopular people.

Not all commercial breaks are crammed with adverts – ITV companies wish that they could be – so gaps where insufficient commercials have been sold are often filled with crisply-edited snippets from programmes which will appear later that day or in days to come. These promotions, as they are called, are more than a stop-gap during a thin commercial break, however. They are a very important part of a television company's output, for a carefully prepared and professionally presented promotion campaign not only makes the viewer aware of what programmes are coming up on his screen, but his appetite for viewing them can be stimulated.

Promotion-writing is a specialised field in television. The writers spend much of their time editing clips from programmes onto video tape, later adding music, captions and the voice of an announcer. There is a strange love-hate relationship between promotion-writers and programme-makers. Every producer and director wants his programme to be promoted as often as possible in the hope that millions will watch when it is being transmitted, but resents bitterly giving up valuable studio, OB or film time in shooting special material for promotions. So promotions are often compiled after programmes have been made, using carefully selected clips backed up by skilful scripts. Throughout ITV the promotion departments of the major companies take it in turns to mount the networked campaigns promoting programmes for the autumn, Christmas, spring, and so on.

The presentation and promotions departments work hand in glove to fill the day's programming; unsung and unknown, they constitute a vital artery in every television company.

It must be mentioned that the presentation department is

concerned with the precise implementation of schedules on a day-to-day basis. The general pattern for the network, however, is worked out and agreed many months before, a pattern which, with few exceptions, all companies are expected to adhere to. Those who work in this important area of programme planning lead a strange life. While ordinary mortals in June look forward to next week's holiday in France, the forward planner is thinking of Christmas.

The careful, long-term, broad thinking of the programme planner, and the precise, last minute flexibility of the presentation executive might appear to oppose each other. The reverse is true, of course. Television must plan ahead, but it must be flexible within controlled limits. Presentation and programme planning make strange, but successful, bedfellows.

Whenever a television programme is being transmitted, a specially made photographic slide containing the name of the programme, usually over a scene which is relevant to it, is loaded into a television slide projector. Should something go wrong with the programme – film breakage, an electronic malfunction, the interruption of signals from an OB – the transmission controller can instantly transmit that slide while an announcer apologises for the loss of the programme, says everything is being done to get it back, and invites the viewer to listen to some music while they wait. Throughout the day as each programme gives way to another, a slide relevant to the new programme moves into place in the projector, ready for instant use. Some companies decree that these continuity (or presentation) announcers are never seen, remaining faceless but familiar voices to the viewers in their area. Others prefer their announcers to be seen, feeling that it humanises the company's relationship with its viewers.

Either way these announcers, working to a shift system, are on duty and on call every second of the transmission day, ready for emergencies, and also for their scripted contributions. It can be a tedious, unrewarding life sometimes, especially for those who are never seen on the home receiver. How often they must wish for something to go wrong bringing some excitement into their working lives!

We referred to photographic slides earlier. These are produced by the stills photography department, a very necessary area in all television companies. This section contributes still photographs needed on television programmes (especially in the news and current affairs area) and they also produce the publicity shots so vital in keeping the company's image before the public.

Few programmes go on location, for example, without a photographer in tow for at least some of the time. Photographs of television crews in action are always interesting to the public, and shots of artistes at work are useful for promotions and publicity. These professional photographers are often responsible for high quality work, and it is remarkable how quickly photographs are taken, developed, enlarged and mounted (or made into slides) to meet the requirements of programme-makers.

Almost a whole book could be written about these vital background areas in television. Many, like the presentation department, are never heard of outside the industry. Others are represented on programme end-credits nightly, although their function may not be fully understood.

Many people, even in television, believe that the graphic artist's sole function is to provide the lettering for the opening titles and closing credits of a programme. Even that calls for much knowledge of type faces and a feeling for the right one to use. An evening spent in front of the television studying the work of the graphic artists, however, will soon reveal just how much they contribute to the visual presentation of programmes. Even on straightforward news bulletins their value is undeniable. We are accustomed to the changing backgrounds behind newsreaders which represent a pictorial interpretation of the story being read. Yet observe, also, the explanatory maps, diagrams, graphs, animated visual explanation of complicated facts, eye-catching layouts of letters and figures – these and many many more are examples of the graphic artists' efforts which are so easily taken for granted. They have moved into electronic realms, too, with the development of exciting equipment, although they still retain the basic skills of their craft which are still called for on many programmes.

Video tape editing is self-explanatory, but with the continuing development of more and more sophisticated equipment it has become almost an art form. Some operators have attained high levels of speed and dexterity indeed, and are much in demand by programme makers. A first-rate editor can assemble a programme to order from a series of apparently unrelated shots and sequences in such a way that not only does the viewer believe that the programme is live, but fellow professionals, knowing the programme to be edited, still cannot 'spot the edits'.

We have touched on the work of such craftsmen as carpenters and painters, whose efforts are so often called for in the creation of make-believe. Their work is usually combined with that of the set constructor, and together they are often responsible for amazingly realistic end-products. Visitors to studios find this aspect of television fascinating, especially when they find, for example, that apparently solid, marble palaces are made from wood and paper combined with brilliant paintwork.

These skills have been developed over many years of experience in theatre and films and are not necessarily peculiar to television, except perhaps in the one area of time. Sets for television programmes rarely spend more than two days in a studio, so they must be easily assembled and dismantled. Paint used on sets and on the floor must be quick-drying and easily removed. Whenever possible, bulky flats are fitted with wheels or castors to enable them to be moved in or out of the studio more easily.

Television, the most technological and electronic of all the media, cannot afford to stand still, and every company has its back-room 'boffins' engaged on the planning, development, installation, smooth running and repair of the millions of components which contribute to the output of television studios. The nerve centre of this electronic nightmare (usually termed Central Apparatus Room, or C.A.R.) usually leaves visitors speechless. Hundreds of cables are enmeshed one with another, their ends vanishing into bays of equipment, or under floorboards which hide what appears to be the aftermath of an explosion in a spaghetti factory. Always, it seems, a white-coated technician is delving into the entrails of C.A.R. or stretched out over an opening in the floor, meter in hand.

It is here, for example, that the connections are made which ensure that when the vision mixer at her desk punches the button marked 'camera one' camera one appears on the screen. There is, however, so much more to the work of the C.A.R. engineers than that, far too complicated to be dealt with here. Probably the simplest way to describe their role is to say that they are responsible for ensuring that the technical side of programme-making functions efficiently, and that the quality of the television pictures and sound emanating from the studios should be the optimum the equipment is capable of.

The rostrum cameraman is a largely anonymous character to the layman, although his work is often seen on television programmes. He operates the camera which provides film shots of still photographs, maps, drawings, painting and so on, especially where smooth and precise movement is required. His camera, loaded with cine film, exposes just one frame at a time; twenty-five frames for every second of 'air time'.

The visual material to be filmed is clamped firmly in place, usually below a downward-pointing camera, and working to the instructions supplied by the director the cameraman programmes his equipment to provide the framing and movement required. One exposure for 0.04 seconds, a miniscule adjustment to the position of the zoom, another 0.04-second exposure, another small adjustment . . . and so it goes on until two hundred exposures later eight seconds of film is available showing for two seconds a shot of a face, then a zoom in to an eye lasting four seconds, with this close-up of the eye held for a further two seconds. Precise and pedantic is the world of the rostrum cameraman, and they now make use of computers which can programme and activate these camera movements.

Those in the front line of television programme-making lead an exciting life, often in the public eye and occasionally touched by glamour and fame. No-one knows more than they, however, just how dependent they are on the skills and application of unsung men with white coats and screwdrivers, girls pounding typewriters, lonely links engineers trying to keep warm on barren hilltops, negative cutters working through the night assembling film they can have no influence over apart from unfailing accuracy, people who 'push paper', who compile schedules allocating space and time in much sought-after studios, who plan the day, the hours, the minute . . . even the 0.04 of a second.

There is room in television for a vast variety of talents and skills. It is a world where there is a high interdependence between these skills, a world where just one man falling down on his responsibilities can lead to the degradation – even the complete destruction – of a programme. For want of a nail . . . !

15 WHAT NOW?

Television has come a long way since John Logie Baird brought the conception, if not the means, of beaming pictures into our living rooms. From its beginnings as a toy for the privileged few, television is arguably now the most potent media in the world. Indeed, there can hardly be anywhere left in the world which has no access to it.

During the 1939–45 war, television, still in its infancy, went to sleep. Such an occurrence just could not happen today. Its influence both as means of entertainment and information is much too powerful to ignore. Despite the criticism, even scorn, which is often pointed at television, it is here to stay, and whether people would admit it or not, its disappearance would be unthinkable.

There have been notable milestones in its comparatively brief life which began in earnest at the Alexandra Palace, affectionately named 'Ally Pally'.

The first must surely have been the birth of commercial television, primarily for the element of competition it introduced into the field. Until then, the BBC had brilliantly pioneered this fragile invention, calling upon its unique knowledge and experience in broadcasting to lead the world in television development. Nevertheless, it operated in a monopolistic environment where film of a potter's wheel or kittens playing with a ball of wool still held viewers entranced in the intervals between programmes, and where the news *in sound only* was accepted without question as a suitable manner in which to end the day's transmissions.

Commercial television, hungry for success and profits, changed all that. It tempted away from the BBC some of its best technicians and programme-makers. It dared to go down-market with many of its programmes. It was bold and brash and it broke new ground and it made mistakes; but it stimulated the industry with its vitality, for the BBC was not slow to match the pace of this young upstart, whilst still retaining its dignity as the pioneer of world television. It took on new staff and trained them.

From now on, every second of transmission time was devoted to the aim of holding the fickle viewer. Television started earlier in the day, and ended later, and there was even television on Sunday afternoons! The commercial break became a fact of life, and the quiz game was here to stay.

The end result, however, was that television, in terms of technique and equipment, took a giant step forward. America, predictably overtaking us in technology and sometimes in ideas, provided a source of stimulation for eager and active programme-makers. The potential of this exciting offspring was beginning to be realised, and the viewing public became less tolerant of mediocrity, even if, paradoxically, it enjoyed the banal.

The second milestone was the development of video tape recording, although its influence was initially felt only within the industry. As we saw earlier, however, it enabled television companies to restructure completely their programme-making techniques, and the advent of video tape editing led to more sophisticated productions, particularly in the field of drama and light entertainment.

The viewer, largely unaware of this development, soon came to enjoy the effect it had on his evenings' programmes. He became accustomed to viewing highlights of sporting occasions within an hour or so of their taking place, for example, and the subtle improvement in the quality of the presentation of programmes was not lost on him.

There is a saying in television that, before the introduction of video tape, 'programmes were made for the ether'. Certainly it is true that many worthwhile programmes were transmitted to the viewer, never to be seen again, and with no tangible record that they ever existed. Video tape changed all that, and now few programmes are committed irrevocably to the ether. There is now more permanence to the programme-maker's art.

Colour television brought a shot in the arm, stimulating viewer interest at a time when complacency was beginning to intrude. For those in the industry, too, it brought new incentives. Formerly the choice of colours to be paraded in front of the camera was conditioned by the shades of grey they would represent on the monochrome receiver. Suddenly, designers and costume-makers could reveal their talents. Lighting directors, make-up artists and technicians faced new challenges and richer rewards.

At last the splendours of state occasion could be enjoyed. Musical spectaculars took on a new richness, and period drama was given the visual icing it deserved. Familiar faces took on a new look, and woe betide the television idol with nicotine-stained fingers. The black and white receiver which had brought so much excitement and drama into our lives suddenly lost its lustre. Colour, without doubt, had taken up permanent residence in the living room.

Since then, the vast leap forward in technology has been mainly the preserve of the professionals. Chroma-key, Quantel, electronic paintboxes and so on have no meaning for the man in the street, but to those in television they offered new opportunities to improve the visual appeal of programmes; the introduction of new techniques to present more stylish television.

For the viewer, however, the next significant innovation must have been the home video recorder, the VCR. At last he was liberated from the confines of the scheduled transmission. No longer did an enforced evening appointment mean the lost chance to view a favourite or long awaited programme, and the infuriating clash between two good programmes on different channels lost its nuisance value. The viewer could record what he wanted, whatever he was doing, and view when he wanted.

As more and more people buy and use VCRs, there is the danger to commercial television that the tendency for viewers to spin through commercial breaks when playing back recordings could have an adverse effect on the selling of advertising time. Who can tell? There is also the fact that many people use their VCRs to view video cassettes instead of transmitted programmes, which might cause programme-makers to look more closely at their own work – not a bad thing.

Events are happening fast in television. By the time this book is printed we shall all be familiar with the varying effects on our lives of satellite and cable television. More and more communities and organisations will have the opportunity to make their own programmes, as is customary in America. The choice of thirty or more channels to choose from will become commonplace for many viewers, as will ordering goods and bank statements via the home receiver. . . .

Looking back, the introduction of BBC 2 and ITV's Channel 4 did not have the initial impact expected. On a long-term basis viewers came to enjoy the opportunities of alternative viewing offered to them, but it was a protracted courtship. With the arrival of Channel 4 and the coming of cable television, however, there has been an increase in the number of independent production companies which are available on hire to programme-makers. Because of the growing popularity of VCRs more and more people are thinking video, and the inventiveness of some of the pop videos is a refreshing outcome of the video explosion. Private firms, travel agencies, overseas property developers and others now look to television 'shorts' to tempt the prospective customer. The increasing popularity of video cameras, too, is making programme-makers of us all.

The obvious lesson from this for all those engaged in professional television is that there can be no standing still. There can be no complacency, no assumption of a captive audience just because one's programme is being transmitted on one of the four main channels. Other forms of video entertainment now compete for the elusive viewer, and this viewer has become more discerning, more demanding regarding the quality of programmes offered to him.

Television, of course, will not stand still. Technically the advances over the past five years alone have been quite staggering, and programme-makers have not been slow to utilise these exciting innovations. Production techniques have expanded and advanced. A newcomer to the industry must really feel that he has the world at his feet.

Behind him he has the backing of decades of experience and experimentation. Ahead of him lie seemingly unlimited opportunities to develop and exploit his craft.

Television, always an exciting, stimulating and rewarding profession, is about to take on new muscle. There is room, as never before, for the talented, the industrious, the inventive, the ambitious. It is a time to be young and to be in television.

INDEX

Figures in italics refer to page numbers of illustrations.